T0330797

Chinese Currency Exchange Rates Analysis

This book provides an overview of Chinese RMB exchange markets and risk management strategies. The view that the RMB is playing an increasingly international role has been widely accepted by practitioners as well as scholars worldwide. Moreover, the Chinese government is opening up control of the RMB exchange market, step by step. However, some related topics are under heated debate, such as how to manage and warn of the currency crisis, what the trend of the RMB exchange rate in the future is, and how to hedge the exchange risk in the process of RMB internationalization. In this book, we will give distinct answers to the above questions.

Jiangze Du is currently Assistant Professor of Finance and Economics at Jiangxi University in China. He obtained his PhD in Management Sciences from City University of Hong Kong in 2015. He specializes in financial time series analysis and financial risk management.

Jying-Nan Wang is currently Professor of Posts and Telecommunications at Chongqing University in China. He obtained his PhD in the Graduate School of Management, Yuan Ze University in 2008. Dr. Wang's research interests are in market microstructure, volatility estimation, and risk management.

Kin Keung Lai received his PhD at Michigan State University, USA. He is currently Professor of Industrial and Manufacturing Systems Engineering at The University of Hong Kong. Professor Lai's main areas of research are operations and supply chain management, as well as financial and business risk analysis.

Chao Wang is currently a PhD candidate in the Department of Management Sciences at City University of Hong Kong. He received his Master's Degree of from Texas A&M University, USA. Chao Wang's main research areas are financial time series analysis and financial risk management.

Routledge Advances in Risk Management
Edited by Kin Keung Lai and Shouyang Wang

For a full list of titles in this series, please visit www.routledge.com/ Routledge-Advances-in-Risk-Management/book-series/RM001

Chinese Currency Exchange Rates Analysis

Risk Management, Forecasting, and Hedging Strategies

Jiangze Du, Jying-Nan Wang, Kin Keung Lai, and Chao Wang

Routledge
Taylor & Francis Group

LONDON AND NEW YORK

First published 2018
by Routledge
2 Park Square, Milton Park, Abingdon, Oxon OX14 4RN

and by Routledge
711 Third Avenue, New York, NY 10017

Routledge is an imprint of the Taylor & Francis Group, an informa business

© 2018 Jiangze Du, Jying-Nan Wang, Kin Keung Lai, and Chao Wang

The right of Jiangze Du, Jying-Nan Wang, Kin Keung Lai, and Chao Wang to be identified as authors of this work has been asserted by them in accordance with sections 77 and 78 of the Copyright, Designs and Patents Act 1988.

British Library Cataloguing in Publication Data
A catalogue record for this book is available from the British Library

Library of Congress Cataloging in Publication Data
A catalog record for this book has been requested

ISBN: 978-1-138-04126-4 (hbk)
ISBN: 978-1-315-17221-7 (ebk)

Typeset in Times New Roman
by diacriTech, Chennai

Contents

Figures

Tables

Preface

With the rapid growth of the Chinese economy during the past several decades, the currency exchange market is becoming increasingly important to China. Since 2006, the Chinese government has begun to take a number of actions to promote the international use of the renminbi (RMB), the Chinese currency. Meanwhile, the liberalization of the renminbi exchange rate is a key step to its internationalization. In fact, the Chinese government is trying to open up the control of its exchange market, step by step. However, topics related to RMB exchange risk management have led to heated debate recently.

This book attempts to answer the following several questions: how to detect and manage currency risk, what the trend of the RMB exchange rate will be in the future, and how to hedge currency risk in the process of the RMB's internationalization. The authors review the related literature and construct theoretical models for the real renminbi exchange market. These models and strategies provide practical guidance for managing and hedging exchange risk based on the analysis and prediction of the currency exchange rate. The details of this book are as follows.

Chapter 1 introduces the overall Chinese currency exchange market from the following three aspects. First, we introduce the development of the Chinese economy in recent years. Second, the development of the Chinese yuan's exchange rate policy is described. Lastly, the Chinese onshore and offshore exchange markets are introduced.

Chapter 2 investigates the interrelationship among the onshore exchange market, the offshore exchange market, and the non-deliverable forward (NDF) market of the RMB using the Johansen cointegration test, the Granger causality test, and vector autoregression (VAR). The empirical results show that a long-term equilibrium relationship exists among these three markets.

Chapter 3 proposes a hybrid Markov switching (MS) method to identify crisis regimes based on different states. The hybrid model is constructed by combining the empirical mode decomposition (EMD) model with the

MS model. The empirical results show that the hybrid model has a similar capacity of predicting currency crisis. However, the proposed hybrid model is more sensitive to currency crisis than the traditional MS model.

Chapter 4 constructs an EMD-MLP model to forecast the RMB exchange rate of different horizons. Based on the constructed model, trading strategies are proposed for the RMB exchange rate. The empirical results reveal that the proposed hybrid EMD-MLP model is more suitable for longer horizons by considering different critical numbers and trading costs.

Chapter 5 studies the importance of hedging RMB exchange-rate risk during the process of the renminbi's internationalization. Both equal and optimal weighted strategies are applied to construct the fully hedged and unhedged portfolios. The empirical results indicate that the fully hedged portfolios perform better than the unhedged portfolios using the criteria of the Sharpe ratio. Moreover, other evidence from efficient frontiers and time-varying rolling estimations indicate that it is necessary to hedge RMB exchange rate risk during its internationalization.

Jiangze DU
School of Finance
Jiangxi University of Finance and
Economics
Nanchang, China
Email: jiangzedu@jxufe.edu.cn

Jying-Nan WANG
School of Economics and Management
Chongqing University of Posts and
Telecommunications
Chongqing, China
Email: jyingnan@gmail.com

Kin Keung LAI
Department of Industrial and
Manufacturing Systems Engineering
The University of Hong Kong
Hong Kong
Email: mskklai@outlook.com

Chao WANG
Department of Management Sciences
City University of Hong Kong
Kowloon, Hong Kong
Email: ccwang6-c@my.cityu.edu.hk

1 Chinese currency exchange market
An overview

1.1 Introduction to Chinese currency exchange market

The *foreign exchange market* is a market in which participants are able to buy, sell, exchange, and speculate on currencies. The foreign exchange market is a major component of the financial market. With the fast development of the economy, China leapfrogged Japan to become the world's second-largest economy in 2011 and became the world's largest economy based on purchasing power parity in 2014, as shown in Figures 1.1 and 1.2. In the meantime, China's government has committed to the reform of the renminbi (RMB) exchange rate regime, where the Chinese currency exchange market has made tremendous development.

Before 1994, China carried out a fixed exchange rate system and a dual-exchange rate system, which contained an official rate for non-trade-related transactions and an internal settlement rate for authorized current account transactions. Then China's government adopted a unified managed floating exchange rate system based on market supply and demand on 1 January 1994. In the ensuing decade, the growth rate of China's economy increased more than 10 percent and the import and export trade grew rapidly. Furthermore, the RMB exchange rate kept basic stability at a reasonable and balanced level, which in turn contributed to maintaining the regional economic and financial stability in the Asian financial crisis. After a successful first phase of development, the Chinese currency exchange market gradually formed.

In order to adapt to economic globalization and RMB internationalization, China moved into another new managed floating exchange rate system in July 2005. That protocol was based on market supply and demand with reference to a basket of currencies, which brought the Chinese currency exchange market a new round of change.

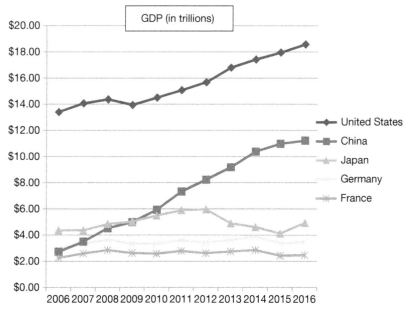

Figure 1.1 GDP in major countries.

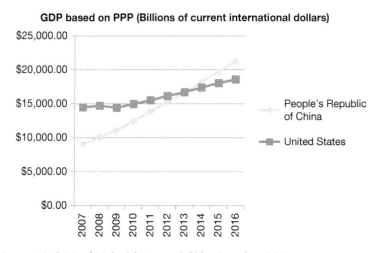

Figure 1.2 GDP of United States and China based on PPP.

Because of the not-fully-open capital account, the Chinese currency exchange market contains two markets: the RMB onshore exchange market and the RMB offshore exchange market. In April 1994, a new interbank system called the China Foreign Exchange Trading System (CFETS) was set up in Shanghai, formally establishing China's interbank foreign exchange market. In 2003, Hong Kong launched personal RMB business. After the revised Clearing Agreement for RMB Business was signed in 2010, the Chinese offshore exchange market in Hong Kong was formally established. The interbank foreign exchange market, the offshore exchange market in Hong Kong, and the major Chinese currency exchange markets have gradually been developed and refined over the past years. The participants of the access threshold, as well as trading types and a clearing and settlement system, have been developed.

At present, the Chinese currency foreign exchange market involves a wide range of transaction types: spot transaction, forward transaction, swap transaction, and other derivative transactions, including foreign exchange option transactions. Non-deliverable forward (NDF) transactions also play a significant role in the offshore exchange market.

Since the reform of the exchange rate regime in 2005, access to the foreign exchange market is not limited to banks and financial institutions; nonbank financial institutions and nonfinancial enterprises can also access the interbank exchange market. Of course, there are fewer restrictions in the offshore market, where Hong Kong residents can also participate in trading.

1.2 The development of the Chinese yuan exchange rate policy

The *exchange rate policy* refers to the measures and methods of a country's monetary authorities to achieve certain policy objectives and the establishment and adjustment of the exchange rate adopted, including two aspects: the choice of exchange rate regime and the adjustment of the exchange rate level.

An exchange rate regime, also called *exchange rate arrangement*, is the way that an authority manages its currency in relation to other currencies and the foreign exchange market. It is closely related to monetary policy and the two are generally dependent on many of the same factors. Since the founding of the People's Republic of China in 1949, the RMB exchange rate regime accompanied by the reform of China's economic system has experienced a tortuous development process. China's economic system has undergone transformations from a

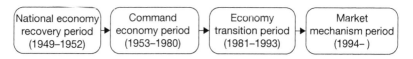

Figure 1.3 The evolution of the Chinese yuan exchange rate regime.

highly centrally planned economy to a socialist market economy since China embarked on its reform and opening-up policy in 1979. As an important part of China's economic system, the RMB foreign exchange system has also undergone transformations from a highly centralized planned management model to the combined plan and market management model, based on foreign exchange retention and a foreign exchange paid system, and then to a model based on supply and demand and a market-oriented management model, which is established on the foreign exchange (FX) sale and purchase system. It is important to consider the evolution of the RMB's exchange rate regime in order to understand the exchange rate policy of the yuan.

Figure 1.3 displays the evolution of the Chinese yuan's exchange rate regime. According to Cui (2014), the evolution of the Chinese Yuan exchange rate regime can be divided into four periods: national economy recovery period (1949–1952), command economy period (1953–1980), economy transition period (1981–1993), and market mechanism period (1994–). These regimes are introduced and discussed in the following sections.

National economy recovery period (1949–1952)

China had experienced a series of wars in the nineteenth century and the early twentieth century until the People's Republic of China was formally established in 1949. During this time, China's government had to issue plenty of banknotes to cover the fiscal deficit, which were used for restoring the national economy. In this situation, China's prices sharply increased and foreign prices remained relatively stable. Also, in order to encourage exports and constrain imports, China's government took a series of measures to cut the RMB exchange rate. Both of these actions by China's government led to the sharp, frequent devaluation of the RMB from 1949 to 1950. The RMB exchange rate continued to appreciate over the next two years. With the national economy stabilizing and the foreign trade policy transferring into balancing imports and exports, China's government increased the RMB exchange rate.

Command economy period (1953–1980)

From the time division in Figure 1.4, we see that the RMB exchange regime in this period can be divided into two phases: the single fixed exchange rate regime from 1953 to 1973, and the pegged exchange rate regime from 1973 to 1980.

In 1953, China entered a new phase of socialist construction and began to carry out a highly centrally-planned economic system in which the government made economic decisions rather than the interactions between consumers and businesses. So, the prices were stable. In the meantime, the RMB exchange rate was pegged to a few currencies of major western countries. Under a typical fixed exchange rate system, devaluation and revaluation are official changes in the value of a country's currency relative to other currencies. But under the Bretton Woods system, countries generally implemented a fixed exchange rate regime, so the RMB exchange rate remained basically unchanged.

Crude oil prices climbed rapidly in the 1970s, soaring from about $3 a barrel in early 1973 to over $35 a barrel in 1980. Global price levels rose and inflation in western countries intensified, directly causing the collapse of the fixed exchange rate regime under the Bretton Woods system. Thus, the currencies of all the industrial countries were set free to float independently. In order to avoid the effects of the recessions in developed countries, China's single fixed exchange rate regime transformed into a pegged exchange rate regime, which was pegged to a currency basket. During this period, the RMB exchange rate fluctuated frequently and was seriously overvalued.

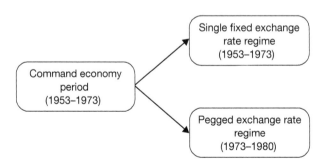

Figure 1.4 The fixed exchange rate regime in the command economy period.

Economy transition period (1981–1993)

From the time that China embarked on its reform and opening-up policy in 1979, the RMB exchange rate regime has transformed from a single official rate to a dual-track system. As Figure 1.5 shows, the dual-track system can also be divided into two phases: the official exchange rate coexisted with the foreign trade-related internal settlement rate period (1981–1984) and the official exchange rate coexisted with the foreign exchange swap market rate period (1985–1993).

In the late 1970s, the overvalued RMB exchange rate depressed the domestic prices of traditional export goods and undermined trading companies' incentive to produce and sell goods in the international market. Therefore, China's government adopted a foreign trade-related internal settlement rate that was set at RMB 2.80 per US dollar, which was calculated on the average cost in terms of foreign exchange for exports plus the 10-percent profit margin. The trade internal settlement rate was applied to all national enterprises and corporations engaging in international trade while the official rate was applied to nontrade transactions. The introduction of the trade-related internal settlement rate reversed the losses of export trade and improved trade balance, but also increased the financial burden and the difficulty of foreign exchange management. So, on 1 January 1985, it was abolished.

In the second phase (1985–1993), the official rate frequently adjusted and depreciated sharply. In order to avoid trade losses caused by inflation and rising prices, the Shenzhen Special Economic Zone set up the first foreign exchange swap center in December 1985, and then all provinces established their own foreign exchange swap centers after March 1988. Through these swap centers, increasing the proportion of foreign

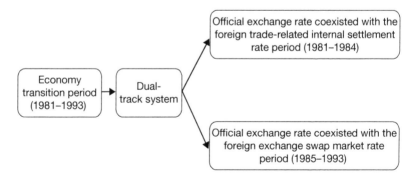

Figure 1.5 The dual-track system in the economy transition period.

exchange retention and expanding the amount of foreign exchange swap reversed the losses of the export trade.

Market mechanism period (1994–)

The official RMB exchange rate and the foreign exchange swap market rate were integrated on 1 January 1994, starting a market-based, managed floating rate system. Similarly, the market mechanism period can be divided into two phases. The two phases with their important events are provided in Figure 1.6.

At the first stage (1994–2005), China introduced a unified managed floating exchange rate regime based on market supply and demand on 1 January 1994. The new exchange rate regime had the following important points. First, the exchange rate was based on market supply and demand. On 1 April 1994, the China Foreign Exchange Trading Center, which implemented match trading and a centralized clearing system, was set up in Shanghai. The exchange rate was managed by the State Administration of Foreign Exchange to keep it at a reasonable level. Also, the RMB was pegged to the dollar for more than a decade starting in 1994. But the daily exchange rate released by the People's Bank of China was floating within the specified range of 120 basis points.

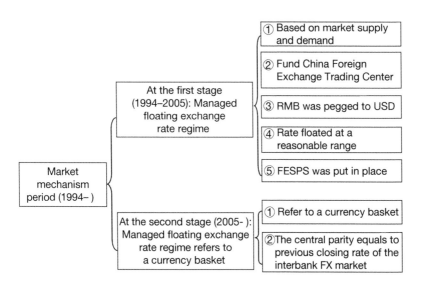

Figure 1.6 Managed floating exchange rate regime in the market mechanism period.

Furthermore, the foreign exchange surrender and purchase system (FESPS) was put in place. The government canceled the retention system and allowed enterprises to participate in free transactions of foreign currencies. In this manner, China's unified interbank foreign exchange market had been established.

At the second stage (2005–), China's government introduced a unified managed floating exchange rate regime based on market supply and demand with reference to a currency basket. Compared to the previous exchange rate regime reform in 1994, the RMB exchange rate no longer pegs only to the USD, but also to a currency basket. Referring to a basket of currencies objectively reduced the volatility of the RMB exchange rate. The People's Bank of China said the central parity was set on a daily basis equal to the closing rate of the interbank foreign exchange market on the previous day.

In summary, the RMB exchange rate regime in this period paid more attention to market supply and demand, which was in line with China's socialist market economy construction. The appropriate exchange rate regime is beneficial to keep the exchange rate stable, promote international trade, and even enhance the comprehensive national strength.

With the deepening of the reform of the RMB exchange rate regime, the RMB embarked on the road to internationalization. In general, for a sovereign currency to become an international currency, it must be experienced as an international trade settlement currency, investment currency, and reserve currency. Now China is already actively promoting greater use of the RMB in other parts of the world, RMB-denominated products have bloomed offshore, and policymakers are opening up the large domestic financial market to foreign investors, which means that RMB is in the stage of investment currency. The specific process of RMB internationalization will be introduced in the following.

Since the late 2000s, China has sought to internationalize its official currency, the RMB. In July 2007, the first dim sum bond was issued in Hong Kong by the China Development Bank; in 2009, the dim sum bond market was established. At the same time, the expanded Cross-Border Trade RMB Settlement Pilot Project was signed, which accelerated the internationalization of the RMB. In 2013, the RMB was the eighth-most traded currency in the world and the seventh-most traded in early 2014. By the end of 2014, the RMB ranked as the fifth-most traded currency. In February 2015, the RMB became the second-most used currency for trade and services, and ranked ninth in FX trading. By the end of 2015, PBOC signed bilateral currency swap agreements with central banks and monetary authorities in 33 countries and regions for a total of 3.3 trillion yuan, promoting not only the development of bilateral trade but also the internationalization of the RMB. The RMB Qualified Foreign Institutional Investor (RQFII) quotas were also extended to six other countries: the UK, Singapore, France, Korea, Germany, and Canada. Previously, only Hong Kong was allowed. Furthermore, the Shanghai Free Trade Zone (SFTZ), which launched in September 2013, and Chinese offshore exchange markets in Hong Kong, Singapore, and London all play a prominent role in the internationalization of the RMB. On 1 October 2016, RMB was added to the IMF's special drawing rights (SDR) basket, joining the US dollar, the euro, the yen, and the British pound. The RMB's inclusion in the SDR basket is an important milestone in the integration of the Chinese economy into the global financial system.

However, there is still a long way to go for the RMB to be considered a reserve currency. Powerful economic strength, strong official and institutional support, and a stable economy in the form of low inflation are all needed to realize RMB internationalization.

1.3 Introduction to Chinese onshore and offshore exchange markets

At present, China's capital account is not fully open, the RMB is not free to convert, and RMB cross-border circulation is still limited. This has led to the development of two markets for the RMB, segregated by a set of regulations governing flows. Figure 1.7 provides the specific divisions of the Chinese foreign exchange (FX) market. Although there is only one Chinese currency, the onshore exchange market (also called CNY market) in mainland China is partly separated from the offshore exchange market (also called CNH market), centered in Hong Kong. The onshore foreign exchange market has many restrictions – for instance, participant base and regulations – that distinguish it from the offshore foreign exchange market.

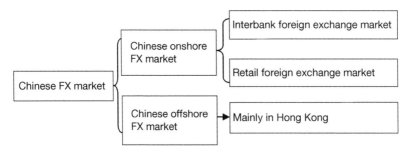

Figure 1.7 The divisions of the Chinese FX market.

The Chinese onshore foreign exchange market is divided into two levels: the interbank foreign exchange market and the retail foreign exchange market between banks and their customers. The retail foreign exchange market is relatively small and fragmented. This section focuses on the interbank foreign exchange market. On 1 April 1994, the China Foreign Exchange Trading Center was set up in Shanghai marking the formation of a unified interbank foreign exchange market. Banks can adjust foreign exchange surplus only at the exchange rate specified by the central bank, so the development of the interbank foreign exchange market has been relatively slow. Since China embarked on a new round of exchange rate regime reform in 2005, the interbank foreign exchange market has also undergone enormous changes, as shown in Figure 1.8.

According to Shu et al. (2015), Figure 1.8 shows several main features of the interbank FX market.

First, interbank foreign exchange market participants (including banks, finance companies, and subsidiaries of foreign banks) are subject to strict restrictions. An obvious feature is that the number of institutions participating in spot foreign exchange transactions is far greater than the number of institutions engaged in foreign exchange derivatives transactions. Second, the CNY market has introduced spot, forward, swap, and options transactions. But among different types of trading, spot contracts and swap contracts account for the majority of transactions, while forward and options transactions account represent a smaller proportion. Furthermore, in 2006 the interbank foreign exchange market introduced the market-maker system and OTC trading, which has provided the market with more liquidity and improved the efficiency of trading. At the same time, netting settlement and central settlement systems have been gradually established.

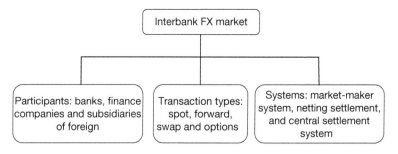

Figure 1.8 The features of the interbank FX market.

On the contrary, the Chinese offshore exchange market has a relatively short history and less intervention. At the end of 2003, Hong Kong launched personal RMB business. Banks in Hong Kong started to offer RMB deposit-taking, currency exchange, remittance, and debit and credit card services to personal accounts on 25 February 2004. Since then, Hong Kong has gradually become the global hub for RMB trade settlement, financing, and asset management, providing a wide range of RMB products and services to investors, businesses, and financial institutions. In 2009, the RMB trade settlement pilot scheme was launched and cross-border trade and settlement started in Hong Kong. Then in July 2010, the revised clearing agreement for RMB business was signed by the People's Bank of China (PBOC) and the Hong Kong Management Association (HKMA). The agreement expanded the scope of the RMB business of the participating banks, allowing banks in Hong Kong to set up RMB deposit accounts for enterprises and other institutions and to transfer freely without trade settlement. These developments marked the beginning of the Chinese offshore exchange market in Hong Kong.

Figure 1.9 shows the features of the offshore market in Hong Kong. Over the years, the range of participants in the Chinese offshore exchange market in Hong Kong has broadened, from the Ministry of Finance of China and banks in mainland China, to financial institutions and hedge funds from different parts of the world. After some aspects of the reform scheme relaxed in 2005, mainland Chinese financial institutions were first allowed to issue offshore RMB bonds in Hong Kong in 2007, and to enterprises from mainland China starting in 2011. At the same time, the range of investors has widened from institutional and private wealth investors to sovereigns, banks, companies, and retail investors.

Also, the offshore exchange market has brought in spot, forward, swap, options, and NDF transactions. Unlike the onshore exchange market, forward exchange transactions and other derivative transactions are more active than spot transactions in the CNH market. CNH rates freely float without restrictions, while CNY rates float within a managed range.

In the meantime, the RMB real-time gross settlement (RTGS) system, a highly efficient and reliable RMB clearing and settlement platform designed by Hong Kong, can facilitate banks from all over the world to make RMB payments. The RMB RTGS system in Hong Kong is linked directly with China's National Advanced Payment System (CNAPS), the high-value RMB payment system in mainland China, enabling RMB transactions with mainland China.

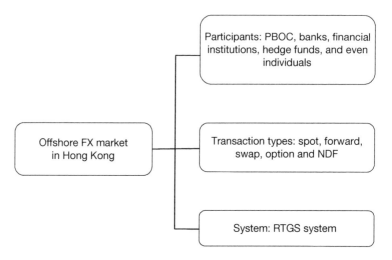

Figure 1.9 The features of the offshore FX market in Hong Kong.

RMB funds in the offshore exchange market derive mainly from cross-border trade settlement. Especially since China expanded the cross-border trade RMB settlement pilot project in 2010, RMB customer deposits and certificate of deposits triggered a rapid acceleration. According to PBOC statistics, by the end of 2014 the main offshore market of RMB deposits reached 1.9867 trillion yuan. In order to enable RMB to be increasingly used, circulated, and accumulated in the overseas markets, PBOC signed a series of bilateral currency swap agreements to provide more liquidity support for the offshore exchange market. At the end of 2015, PBOC had signed bilateral currency swap agreements with central banks and monetary authorities in 33 countries and regions for a total of 3.3 trillion yuan. China has also developed the ways of RMB return of capital including the dim sum bond market, RMB cross-border direct investment settlement, and RMB Qualified Foreign Institutional Investors (RQFII), which has strengthened cross-border RMB flows and promoted RMB internationalization.

Of course, as the RMB plays an increasingly important role in the international financial market, the Chinese offshore exchange market is not limited to the Hong Kong offshore market. Singapore, London, and New York and other regions have also established their own RMB offshore centers. The expansion of the Chinese offshore exchange market has also boosted RMB internationalization. In other words, the Chinese onshore exchange market and offshore exchange market will continue to coexist before China's capital account is fully open. At the same time, China's government should coordinate these two markets to serve the economy.

2 Interrelationship between RMB markets

2.1 Introduction

As the renminbi's internationalization accelerates, the RMB pricing market has developed into the following areas: the CNY market, the CNH market, and the NDF market. The *CNY market* is based on the onshore RMB (CNY), deliverable in mainland China. The *CNH market* is based on delivery of the offshore RMB; at present, Hong Kong, London, and Singapore each have an established center for the CNH. Finally, the *NDF market* refers to a CNH-based non-deliverable forward, relative to the CNY and settled in US dollars. Studies on the CNH market, which is relatively new, are few. Although there is some papers written about the RMB market, they mainly concentrate on the CNY and NDF markets. During the internationalization of RMB, knowing the relations between CNY, CNH, and NDF markets and how they influence each other is necessary, which not only reflects the market pattern of the RMB exchange rate, but also provides market participants such as hedgers, speculators, arbitrageurs, and regulators with beneficial information.

When it comes to the literature related to these three markets, most focus on only two of them. For instance, the relationship between CNY and NDF markets around the exchange reform period has been studied by Huang and Wu (2006), in which they propose CNY leads at both one month and one year. However, only the one-month NDF leads CNY, while the one-year NDF does not lead CNY. By surveying the dynamic linkage of the offshore NDF market and the onshore forward exchange market, Yan and Ba (2010) find that NDF is the center of market price information. To be specific, the pricing leading power of NDF is stronger than both the spot market and onshore forward markets. Since the fourth quarter of 2010, the correlation between CNH spot price and CNY spot price has risen sharply, shown in Prasad and Ye (2011). More studies about the dynamic relationship between these three markets are listed in the last part of this chapter. However, since the last RMB exchange rate reform, we have not found a complete and detailed description about the relationships between these three markets in the above papers, including those listed in the references. Thus, based on the latest data (ranging from August 2010 to December 2013) of three different RMB markets, this chapter studies the interrelationship of these three markets. And we adopt the methodology of the vector autoregression model which is used to test whether there are existing long-run equilibrium relationships between these markets. In addition, we describe the dynamic relationship by estimating the vector autoregressive model and attempt to identify the guiding or the lag factor.

The remainder of this chapter is organized as follows. A description of the methodology, mainly based on the vector autoregression model, is provided in Section 2.2, and Section 2.3 presents empirical results and related explanation. Finally, the conclusions drawn from this chapter are presented in Section 2.4.

2.2 Methodology (vector autoregression model)

The flowchart for time series analysis about the equilibrium relationship is shown in Figure 2.1. To study the long-run relationships between the CNY market, CNH market, and NDF market, the experimental time series are required to be stationary in this chapter, where the stationarity of time series is examined by carrying out a unit root test. The augmented Dickey–Fuller (ADF) unit root test is widely used in many studies to test the stationarity of time series data. First, we need to test the stationarity of the experimental time series. If the test results show that the time series has unit roots, the time series is not stationary and first-order differencing needs to be done. Then the new time series, which is processed by first-order difference action, is tested again until we get a stationary time series for the next analysis by repeating the above steps. Secondly, we apply the Johansen cointegration test to investigate the cointegration of these time series. In general, if two or more time series are individually integrated in terms of the time series sense and some linear combination of them has a lower order of integration, then these time series are said to be cointegrated. Similarly, we should analyze the result of the cointegration test to determine whether it is important. If the test result is significant – showing that a long-run equilibrium relationship exists between these time series – then the detailed regression equation of the time series will be estimated in the next step.

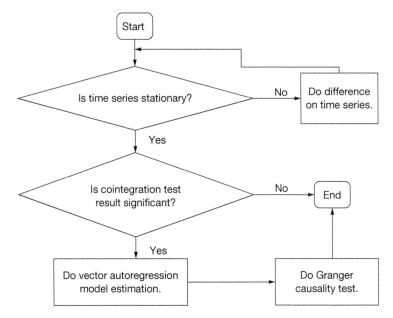

Figure 2.1 Flowchart for analysis of time series about equilibrium
relationship.

However, we will end the analysis if the test result is not significant,
which indicates there is no long-run equilibrium relationship between
these time series.

Third, we introduce the vector autoregression model to estimate
the long-run equilibrium relationship. Finally, we conduct the Granger
causality test for the time series, which is used to examine whether a
causal relationship exists between these experimental time series and
further indicates the guiding factor or the guided factor.

Now, a detailed description of the vector autoregression (VAR)
model is provided. We can use VAR, which is a statistical model, to cap-
ture the linear interdependencies among multiple time series; the univar-
iate autoregression (AR) models are extended by VAR models, allowing
for more than one evolving variable. Though the estimated response
coefficients are usually not the same in terms of structure, all VAR variables are treated symmetrically and, based on its own lags and the lags
of other variables, each variable has an equation that is used to explain
its evolution. The only prior knowledge required for VAR modeling is a
list of variables that can be assumed to be intertemporally interdepend-
ent, which is different from the structural models with simultaneous

equations that require as much knowledge about the forces influencing a variable as possible. The evolution of a set of k endogenous variables over the same sample period ($t = 1...T$) is described as a linear function of only their past values in a VAR model. A *pth* order VAR, expressed as $VAR(p)$, is

$$y_t = c + A_1 y_{t-1} + A_2 y_{t-2} + ... + A_p y_{t-p} + e_t \tag{2.1}$$

Where A_i is a time invariant $k * k$ matrix a, y_t is the observation variable and e_t is a $k * 1$ vector of error terms satisfying that $E[e_t] = 0, E[e_t e_t'] = \Omega, E[e_t e_{t-k}'] = 0$. Besides, a *pth*-order VAR is also called a VAR with p lags. Since the reasoning depends on the correctness of the selected lag order, we should pay more attention to the process of selecting the maximum lag p in the VAR model. In our case, if the test result of the cointegration test is significant, then we apply the VAR model to estimate the relationships between the three time series – that is, CNH, CNY, and NDF, where the variables CNH, CNY, and NDF are respectively defined as $y_{1,t}$, $y_{2,t}$, and $y_{3,t}$. In the meantime, we use $y_1(-i)$ to denote *ith* lag for the CNH variable, $y_2(-i)$ to denote *ith* lag for the CNY variable, and $y_3(-i)$ to denote *ith* lag for the NDF variable. Then the P lags VAR model for these three time series variables can be denoted as,

$$
\begin{aligned}
y_{1,t} = {} & c_1 + A_{1,1} y_1(-1) + A_{1,2} y_1(-2) + \cdots \\
& + A_{1,p} y_1(-p) + A_{1,p+1} y_2(-1) + A_{1,p+2} y_2(-2) + \cdots \\
& + A_{1,2p} y_2(-p) + A_{1,2p+1} y_3(-1) + A_{1,2p+2} y_3(-2) + \cdots \\
& + A_{1,3p} y_3(-p) + \varepsilon_1
\end{aligned} \tag{2.2}
$$

$$
\begin{aligned}
y_{2,t} = {} & c_2 + A_{2,1} y_1(-1) + A_{2,2} y_1(-2) + \cdots \\
& + A_{2,p} y_1(-p) + A_{2,p+1} y_2(-1) + A_{2,p+2} y_2(-2) + \cdots \\
& + A_{2,2p} y_2(-p) + A_{2,2p+1} y_3(-1) + A_{2,2p+2} y_3(-2) + \cdots \\
& + A_{2,3p} y_3(-p) + \varepsilon_2
\end{aligned} \tag{2.3}
$$

$$
\begin{aligned}
y_{3,t} = {} & c_3 + A_{3,1} y_1(-1) + A_{3,2} y_1(-2) + \cdots \\
& + A_{3,p} y_1(-p) + A_{3,p+1} y_2(-1) + A_{3,p+2} y_2(-2) + \cdots \\
& + A_{3,2p} y_2(-p) + A_{3,2p+1} y_3(-1) + A_{3,2p+2} y_3(-2) + \cdots \\
& + A_{3,3p} y_3(-p) + \varepsilon_3
\end{aligned} \tag{2.4}
$$

According to VAR lag order selection criteria in the software program EViews, including the Akaike information criterion (AIC), the Schwarz information criterion (SC), and the Hannan–Quinn information criterion

(HQ), we need to choose the optimal lag length of VAR equations which most of the criteria suggest. We should obey the rule that the minority is subordinate to the majority if the suggestions are not uniform. And then, based on the above system equations, we perform the related VAR models to estimate the long-run equilibrium relationship between the CNH, CNY, and NDF time series.

2.3 Empirical results

We downloaded the data, including the daily settlement exchange rate of the CNH, CNY, and NDF from 24 August 2010 to 3 December 2013, from the Bloomberg database, totaling 846 observations. The exchange rate of the CNH, CNY, and NDF is shown in Figure 2.2 at a conventional scale, where the vertical axis represents the exchange rate value, and the horizontal axis represents the observation numbers. By analyzing the coordinate diagram in detail, we can find that the average of these three exchange rate markets is very close, where CNY is a little larger than CNH, and NDF is a little bit above CNY. If we apply statistical

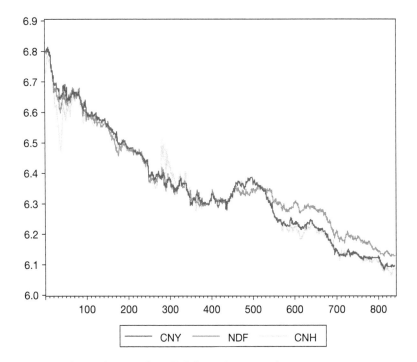

Figure 2.2 CNH, CNY, and NDF daily settlement exchange rate.

software to deal with the data of these exchange rates, it is obvious that their descriptive statistics have positive skewness and kurtosis rather than normal distribution.

First, based on Table 2.1, which presents the ADF test results on these three CNH, CNY, and NDF markets, we cannot reject the null hypothesis because the significance value is greater than 5 percent. Null hypothesis is the individual unit root process that exists among the data of these exchange rates, which means that our exchange rate data have an individual unit root process. From the intermediate result of Table 2.2, we see that all three series have unit root processes, which indicates these time series for exchange rate data are nonstationary. According to the methodology introduced in Section 2.2, we can conduct the cointegration test only if the experimental time series are stationary. Therefore, we do first order difference on these nonstationary time series and use the ADF unit root test to test these new time series processed by first order difference action. Repeat the above steps until we get stationary time series. The ADF unit root test results in first-order difference of CNH, first-order difference of CNY, and first-order difference of NDF are presented in Table 2.3, where the significance value is almost zero. So, the null hypothesis

Table 2.1 ADF unit root test on CNY, CNH and NDF.

Method	Statistic	Prob.**
ADF - Fisher Chi-square	10.8189	0.0941
ADF - Choi Z-stat	−1.53842	0.0620

Table 2.2 Intermediate ADF test results.

Series	Prob.	Series	Prob.
CNY	0.1007	D(CNH)	0.0000
NDF	0.0943	D(CNY)	0.0000
CNH	0.4712	D(NDF)	0.0000

Table 2.3 ADF unit root test on D(CNY), D(CNH), and D(NDF).

Method	Statistic	Prob.**
ADF - Fisher Chi-square	483.570	0.0000
ADF - Choi Z-stat	−21.4509	0.0000

should be rejected and we can conclude that there is no unit root process existing among these three first-order difference time series, based on the intermediate result of Table 2.2. To be more specific: all of CNH, CNY, and NDF are first-order integrated time series variables defined as $I(1)$, where stationary time series $I(0)$ is their first-order difference.

The null hypothesis shows that the individual unit root process does exist among these time series. ** denotes that probabilities for Fisher tests are computed using an asymptotic chi-square distribution. All other tests assume asymptotic normality.

Second, we need to test the long-run relationships between these time series by applying the cointegration test. The Johansen test, as the description of methodology in Section 2.2 states, is a procedure for testing the cointegration of several $I(1)$ time series, which permits more than one cointegrating relationship. Now we use the software program EViews to perform the Johansen cointegration test. The Johansen cointegration test results for the three exchange markets are shown in Table 2.4, where the effect of the Johansen tests with trace and the Johansen tests with eigenvalue are similar. As previously stated, the null hypothesis means that there is no cointegration relationship between the time series for exchange rate, and Table 2.4 displays that the unrestricted cointegration rank test rejects the hypothesis at the 5-percent level, which indicates that these three exchange markets have a long-run equilibrium relationship. Then we use the unrestricted cointegration rank test indicating one cointegrating equation at the 5-percent level to describe the equilibrium relationship. Actually, apart from an integrated equation, if we examine the normalized cointegration coefficients of separated equations, we will find that the separate interrelationships exist in any two of the three exchange rate markets, that is, each two of the three exchange rate markets have an equilibrium relationship.

Third, we use the vector autoregression (VAR) model to estimate the long-run equilibrium relationship between these three markets. Therefore, we should choose the optimal lag length of VAR equations

Table 2.4 Johansen cointegration test on CNH, CNY, and NDF.

Hypothesized CE(s)	No. of Eigenvalue	Trace Statistic	0.05 Critical value	Prob.**
None *	0.033899	44.18218	29.79707	0.0006
At most 1	0.014787	15.17903	15.49471	0.0557
At most 2	0.003147	2.650401	3.841466	0.1035

first, then conduct the VAR test. Based on the result of several VAR lag order selection criteria shown in Table 2.5 (including AIC, SC, and HQ criteria), we find that AIC selects four lags as optimal lag length while SC and HQ criteria select two lags as the optimal length. Then, according to the rule that the minority is subordinate to the majority, the optimal lag length of VAR equations first should be two lags. The estimated results for the VAR model are provided in Table 2.6 where

Table 2.5 VAR lag order selection criteria.

Lag	LogL	AIC	SC	HQ
0	4217.054	−10.02153	−10.00464	−10.01506
1	8967.411	−21.29705	−21.22950	−21.27116
2	9041.163	−21.45104	−21.33282*	−21.40573*
3	9050.692	−21.45230	−21.28341	−21.38757
4	9067.344	−21.47050*	−21.25094	−21.38635
5	9072.643	−21.46170	−21.19147	−21.35813

Table 2.6 Vector autoregression estimates.

	CNH	CNY	NDF
CNH(−1)	**0.762349**	−0.051147	−0.035373
	(0.04430)	(0.03069)	(0.03406)
	[17.2073]	[−1.66648]	[−1.03865]
CNH(−2)	0.223827	0.051286	0.063298
	(0.05692)	(0.03943)	(0.04376)
	[3.93209]	[1.30055]	[1.44657]
CNY(−1)	−0.014989	**0.791255**	0.050057
	(0.05995)	(0.04153)	(0.04608)
	[−0.25003]	[19.0532]	[1.08627]
CNY(−2)	0.129074	0.125126	0.080445
	(0.07622)	(0.05280)	(0.05859)
	[1.69353]	[2.36986]	[1.37309]

(*continued*)

Table 2.6 Vector autoregression estimates (*continued*)

	CNH	CNY	NDF
NDF(−1)	**0.499408**	**0.273757**	**0.971376**
	(0.05817)	(0.04030)	(0.04472)
	[8.58536]	[6.79339]	[21.7237]
NDF(−2)	**−0.563531**	**−0.251790**	−0.164237
	(0.07371)	(0.05106)	(0.05666)
	[−7.64512]	[−4.93087]	[−2.89855]
C	0.048898	0.026667	0.065196
	(0.01874)	(0.01298)	(0.01440)
	[2.60971]	[2.05446]	[4.52652]
R-squared	0.996901	0.998621	0.997798

each column denotes the coefficient for each exchange rate market, for instance, the coefficients of the VAR model for the CNH time series are in the first column. In the meantime, we also give the estimated errors and t statistics value in parentheses and square brackets under each coefficient in Table 2.6. Furthermore, we can explore some other useful results by analyzing the particular value of coefficients of the VAR model. We find that the main explanation for the CNH date is composed of the three components including CNH first lag value, NDF first lag value, and NDF second lag value, where both the CNH first lag value and NDF first lag value have some positive effects on the CNH variable while the NDF second lag value has some negative effects on the CNH variable. The first lag of the CNY exchange rate, first lag of the NDF exchange rate, and second lag of the NDF exchange rate consist of the main explanation for the value of the CNY exchange rate, where both the CNY first lag value and NDF first lag value have some positive effects on the CNY variable while the NDF second lag value has some negative effects on the CNY variable. However, the value of the NDF exchange rate is mainly explained by only its first lag value. Therefore, we can draw a conclusion that the CNH and CNY exchange rate markets are influenced much by the NDF market while the NDF market is relatively more independent, which is not influenced by both the CNY and CNH markets.

Besides, we can get the R square values for each VAR equation in the last row of Table 2.6. Through analyzing the results of R square values, we can find that all R square values in three different markets are close to one, indicating that these VAR equations have good adaptability and are able to deal with the data very well.

In order to better understand the interrelationships between the CNY, CNH, and NDF markets and the characteristics of the whole system, we introduce impulse response functions, which are widely used in contemporary macroeconomic modeling, to investigate how each time series responds to the shocks of the other two time series in our study. Impulse response functions, usually called shocks by economists, are used to describe how the economy reacts over time to exogenous impulses and often modeled in the context of a vector autoregression. Figure 2.3 presents the impulse response of CNH, CNY, and NDF. As shown in the first plotted figure, CNY and NDF have a positive impact on CNH. NDF can make CNH rise nearly 30 points after the first period and then gradually decline to zero, and CNY can make CNH rise gradually from the beginning and close to 30 points. Based

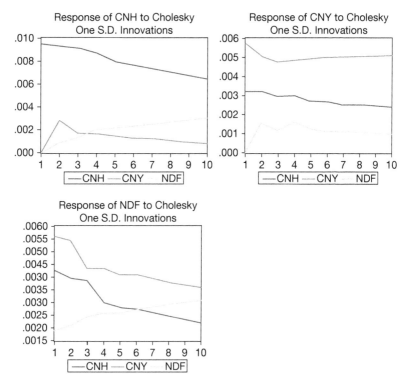

Figure 2.3 Impulse response of CNH, CNY, and NDF.

on the second plotted figure, we can find that for CNY, only NDF has a positive impact, while CNH has a negative impact on CNY. Similarly, NDF makes CNY rise nearly 30 points after the first period and then drop slightly before returning to 30 points after the third period, then gradually declining to zero. In the third plotted figure, it is easy to distinguish the different impacts of CNY and CNH on NDF, based on different trendlines. CNH has a negative impact on NDF while CNY has a positive impact on NDF.

Finally, we apply the Granger causality test to examine whether there is a causal relationship between these experimental time series and further indicate the guiding factor or the guided factor. We have known that these three exchange rate markets have a long-run equilibrium relationship via VAR model estimation. However, we only know that there is a long-run equilibrium relationship between time series rather than the specific impact process between variables. In other words, we introduce the Granger causality test to analyze whether one of the two variables can Granger cause the other, i.e. whether one time series is useful in forecasting another. The Granger causality principle is defined as follows: if a time series X can be shown to Granger cause Y, usually through a series of t-tests and F-tests on lagged values of X and lagged values of Y, that the X values provide statistically significant information about future values of Y.

The results of the Granger causality test are provided in Table 2.7. Significant probability is assumed strictly as 1 percent in our study. From the first two lines, the significant probability that CNY does not Granger cause CNH is 0.01 percent, which indicates that CNY Granger causes CNH. However, the significant probability that CNH does not Granger cause CNY is far greater than 1 percent, indicating that CNH

Table 2.7 Granger causality tests.

Null Hypothesis	F-Statistic	Prob.
CNY does not Granger cause CNH	5.74208	0.0001
CNH does not Granger cause CNY	0.67313	0.6107
NDF does not Granger cause CNH	23.8949	1.E-18
CNH does not Granger cause NDF	2.91576	0.0206
NDF does not Granger cause CNY	13.9817	5.E-11
CNY does not Granger cause NDF	4.33549	0.0018

does not Granger cause CNY. In a similar manner, from the result in the third and fourth rows, we can find that NDF Granger causes CNH, while CNH does not Granger cause NDF. Based on the last two lines, we can see that NDF and CNY Granger cause each other. Apart from the case of CNY Granger causing NDF, the conclusion of all these three parts is consistent with the conclusions drawn from the VAR model. When we attempt to explain the model result coefficient, we can use the threshold setting difference to explain the exception.

2.4 Conclusion

In this chapter, we studied the interrelationships between the CNY, CNH, and NDF exchange rate markets. First, in order to verify there are long-term equilibrium relationships between these three markets, we introduced the Johansen cointegration test. We also used a linear equation to simulate their interrelationships and also to find whether a long-term equilibrium relationship exists between any two of these three markets.

CNY has a relatively positive influence on the CNH exchange rate market based on the impulse response test. Then, we applied the VAR model to further estimate the interrelationships between these three markets. The results of the VAR model estimation show that the NDF market has important impacts on the CNH and CNY exchange rate markets, while the NDF market is not severely influenced by both the CNH and CNY markets. To be more specific, in addition to being affected by their first lag values, the current period data of CNY and CNH is also affected by the first lag of NDF data and the NDF second lag value. Furthermore, based on the impulse response test, we also find that CNY has a relatively positive impact on the CNH exchange rate market.

Finally, from the results of the Granger causality test, we can conclude that both the CNY and NDF markets Granger cause the CNH market while CNH does not Granger cause the NDF and CNY markets. Besides, because the significant probability of NDF does not Granger cause CNH or CNY, it is much smaller than the significant probability that CNY does not Granger cause CNH or NDF, so the NDF variable is regarded as a guiding factor.

3 Chinese exchange market crisis

Warning and identification based on Markov regime switching model

3.1 Introduction

Since 2005, the Chinese government has been pushing the internationalization of the RMB and liberalizing the CNY, which resulted in increased currency volatility and a higher frequency of currency crises. The 1997 Asian currency crisis and 2008 American subprime crisis are the most influential financial crises since 1990. It is significant to establish and improve the investigation of identifying a pre-crisis regime, not only for policymakers but also for financial institutions. In this chapter, the Markov switching model will be used to solve this problem for Chinese currency market.

In 1989, Hamilton developed the Markov switching model. Since then, this model has been widely used and expanded in detecting a financial crisis. Before the Markov switching model, many other approaches were used by academic researchers to develop a warning system for currency crises. For example, by monitoring the evolution of selected macroeconomic variables exhibiting unusual behavior, Kaminsky, Lizondo, and Reinhart (1998) developed the well-known warning system for currency crises. According to the results, they calculated the possibility of experiencing a crisis within the next 24 months. Berg and Pattillo (1999) modified and applied the probit model to construct a pre-warning system. The improved probit model was a contrast to the signal approach which was proposed by Kaminsky et al. (1998). One of the shortcomings of these studies, however, is that they assumed the pre-crisis regime had a fixed length, such as 24 months or 48 months. Actually, the financial pre-crisis was more complicated than they assumed and the fixed length was unrealistic. Therefore, overcoming the shortcomings by applying the Markov switching model to determine the financial regime endogenously is the most important part of this chapter.

Some scholars have already applied the Markov switching model to detect a currency crisis. In order to access the vulnerable macroeconomic condition and contagion effect in Indonesia, Cerra and Saxena (2002) introduced the Markov switching model with time-varying transition probabilities. Abiad (2003) developed an early crisis warning system, based on the Markov switching model, which was used for analyzing the East Asian financial system. Also, the three-states Markov switching model, in which they defined a moderately vulnerable regime as between a tranquil regime and crisis regime, was applied by Chen (2006) to research the East Asian crisis.

The results of the above studies show that, compared with traditional constant probabilities and two regimes, the Markov switching model, with time-varying transition probabilities or three regimes, has no significant advantage. Furthermore, the three-state Markov switching model and the time-varying transition probabilities are not only computationally complex, but also hard to get convergent results in out-of-sample evaluation. In order to avoid the above two situations, the Markov switching model with constant transition probabilities and two regimes are chosen in this chapter.

The rest of this chapter is organized as follows. Section 3.2 introduces the methodology related to the Markov switching EMD method. Section 3.3 describes the model specification and estimation in detail. The empirical analysis and results are displayed in Section 3.4, and Section 3.5 concludes this chapter.

3.2 Methodology

3.2.1 Markov switching model

The Markov switching model is a flexible specification in the process of world heterogeneous state-driven processing. A concise exposition on the Markov switching models is given in this section. More thorough and technical details about the Markov switching model can be found in Hamilton (1994).

Consider the following process given by:

$$y_t = \mu_{S_t} + \epsilon_t \tag{3.1}$$

A first-order Markov chain, $S_t = 1...k$, followed by y_t, which is the dependent variable, and ϵ_t follows a normal distribution, with zero mean and variance given by $\delta_{S_t}^2$. Note that for the model given in Equation 3.1, the intercept and variance portions switch their values relative to the indicator variable S_t, which means that if there are k states, then μ and $\delta \wedge 2$ will have k values. Certainly, when there is only one state, Equation 3.1 will be a simple linear regression model.

For our cases, the model has two states ($k = 2$). Therefore, an alternative representation is:

$$y_t = \mu_1 + \epsilon_t \quad \text{for state 1} \tag{3.2}$$

$$y_t = \mu_2 + \epsilon_t \quad \text{for state 2} \tag{3.3}$$

Where:
For state 1, $\epsilon_t \sim (0, \delta_1^2)$
For state 2, $\epsilon_t \sim (0, \delta_2^2)$

Two different processes for the dependent variable y_t are clearly implied in this representation. When the state of the world for time t is 1, then the expectation of the dependent variable is μ_1 and the volatility of the innovations is δ_1^2. Similarly, the expectation and the volatility will be μ_2 and δ_2^2 respectively when t is 2.

For an empirical example, y_t could be expressed as a vector of log returns for a financial asset. The expected log return on a bull market state is the assumed higher value of μ_1, which means a positive trend of the financial prices and thus a positive log return for y_t. In contrast, the expected log return for the bear market state is the assumed lower value of μ_2, which means a negative trend in financial prices and a negative log return for y_t. In our studies, y_t, the dependent variable, represents the market pressure index, which is calculated from the value of the exchange rate series and international reserve series. The assumed higher value of δ_1^2 implies higher volatility and usually denotes a crisis state, while lower volatility and a tranquil state are accompanied by an assumed lower value of δ_2^2. In a later section of this chapter, these specifications are introduced in detail. Generally, the S_t variable simply denotes the states with the interpretation given by looking at the parameter's value. How to exactly switch from one state to the other is discussed in the following. For instance, how does one know the state at each point in time? When an exogenous time series z_t is positive, we suppose that the assumed deterministic transition of states where state 1 is true for time t, which will greatly simplify the model. With each state being observable, the model with dummy variables given beforehand can be treated as a regression.

This would take the shape of $y_t = D_t(\mu_1 + \epsilon_{1,t}) + (1 - D_t)(\mu_2 + \epsilon_{1,t})$, where D_t is the dummy variable that takes value of 1 if z_t is positive and 0 otherwise. However, for the Markov switching model, the transition of states is random rather than deterministic, which implies that we are never sure whether there will be a switch of state or not. However, the dynamics behind the switching process are known. A transition matrix, the switching process driven by it, controls the probabilities of making a switch from one state to the other.

It can be represented as:

$$P = \begin{bmatrix} p_{11} & \cdots & p_{1k} \\ \vdots & \ddots & \vdots \\ p_{k1} & \cdots & p_{kk} \end{bmatrix}$$

The probability of a switch from state j to state i is controlled by the element in row i, column $j (p_{ij})$. For instance, the element in p_{12} means the probability of a switch from state 2 to state 1 between time t and time $t + 1$ where state is 2 at time t. Likewise, p_{22} determines the probability of staying in state 2.

In short, the switching of the states itself is a random process, which is one of the central points of the structure of a Markov switching model. For the sake of convenience, the probabilities of transition often are assumed constant. A time-varying transition probabilities model means that the probabilities of transition are allowed to vary over time; this is quite intricate and not introduced in our empirical study.

Given the state $S_t = j$ at time t, assuming that the conditional density of y_t is:

$$f(y_t \mid S_t = j, y_{t-1};\theta) \tag{3.4}$$

Where θ is a vector of parameters that includes the parameters, which characterize the conditional density of y_t. For our cases, $\theta = (\mu_1, \mu_1, \delta_1^2, \delta_2^2, p_{11}, p_{22})$.

If there are N different states, then there are N conditional densities. These densities are collected in a $N * 1$ vector η_t:

$$\eta_t = \begin{bmatrix} f(y_t \mid S_t = 1, y_{t-1};\theta) \\ \vdots \\ f(y_t \mid S_t = N, y_{t-1};\theta) \end{bmatrix} \tag{3.5}$$

If the conditional density assumes a normal distribution, then the *jth* element of the above vector will be:

$$\eta_{jt} = f(y_t \mid s_{t=j}, \theta) = \frac{1}{\sqrt{2\pi}\sigma_j} \exp(\frac{-(y_t - \mu_j)^2}{2\sigma_j^2}) \tag{3.6}$$

3.2.2 Empirical mode decomposition (EMD)

Empirical mode decomposition (EMD), which decomposes a data series into a number of intrinsic mode functions (IMFs), was proposed by Huang et al. (1998) and Huang, Shen, and Long (1999). It is designed for nonstationary and nonlinear datasets. In order to apply EMD, time series datasets must meet two conditions in the following.

For each local maximum and local minimum, there must be one zero crossing following up. To be specific, the sum of local maxima and local minima must be equal to the total number of zero crossings, or the difference between them is one. Only when the average of the upper envelope (defined by the local maximum) and the lower envelope (defined by the local minimum) is zero, can the local average be zero. Therefore, an IMF function represents a signal that is symmetric to the local mean zero. Furthermore, an IMF, whose frequency and amplitude can change, is a simple oscillatory mode that is more general than the simple harmonic function.

Then, data series $x(t)$ ($t = 1, 2, ..., n$) can be decomposed by the following sifting procedure.

First, find all local maxima and minima in $x(t)$. Then the upper envelope $x_{up}(t)$ and lower envelope $x_{low}(t)$ will be generated by using the cubic spline line to respectively connect all local maxima and all local minima.

According to the upper and lower envelopes obtained in Step 1, calculate the envelope mean $m_1(t)$:

$$m_1(t) = (x_{up}(t) + x_{low}(t)) / 2 \tag{3.7}$$

1 Data series $x(t)$ minus envelope mean $m_1(t)$ gives the first component $d_1(t)$:

$$d_1(t) = x(t) - m_1(t) \tag{3.8}$$

2 Check if $d_1(t)$ satisfies the IMF requirements: if $d_1(t)$ does not, go back to Step 1 and replace $x(t)$ with $d_1(t)$ to conduct the second sifting procedure, i.e., $d_2(t) = d_1(t) - m_2(t)$. Repeat the sifting procedure k times $d_k(t) = d_{k-1}(t) - m_k(t)$ until the following stop criterion is satisfied:

$$\sum_{t=1}^{T} \frac{[d_j(t) - d_{j+1}(t)]^2}{d_j^2(t)} < SC \tag{3.9}$$

where SC is the stopping condition. Normally, it is set between 0.2 and 0.3. Then, we get the first IMF component, i.e., $c_1(t) = d_k(t)$.

1   Subtract the first IMF component $c_1(t)$ from data series $x(t)$ and get the residual $r_1(t) = x(t) - c_1(t)$.

2   Treat $r_1(t)$ as the new data series and repeat Steps 1 through 3. Then get the new residual $r_2(t)$. In this way, after repeating n times, we get:

$$r_2(t) = r_1(t) - c_2(t)$$
$$r_3(t) = r_2(t) - c_3(t)$$

$$.$$
$$.$$ (3.10)
$$.$$

$$r_n(t) = r_{n-1}(t) - c_n(t)$$

When the residual $r_n(t)$ becomes a monotonic function, the data sets cannot be decomposed anymore. The whole EMD is completed. The original data series can be described as the combination of n IMF components and a mean trend $r_n(t)$:

$$x(t) = \sum_{j=1}^{n} c_j(t) + r_n(t)$$ (3.11)

In this way, the original data series $x(t)$ can be decomposed into n IMFs, which are used for instantaneous frequency analysis and a mean trend function. The traditional Fourier transform decomposes a data series into a number of sine or cosine waves for the analysis. However, the EMD technique decomposes the data series into several sinusoid-like signals with variable frequencies and a mean trend function.

Compared with the traditional Fourier transform decomposing a data series into a number of sine or cosine waves for the analysis, the EMD technique, which decomposes the data series into several sinusoid-like signals with variable frequencies and a mean trend function, has following advantages.

First, comparatively speaking, because of its simpler mathematical algorithms, the EMD technique is easier to understand and is widely used. Second, it's more appropriate to deal with nonlinear and nonstationary data series with EMD. Third, applying the EMD technique to analyze data series with trends, such as economic and weather data, is more appropriate. Finally, the residual revealing the data series with trends can be found by applying the EMD technique described by Yu et al. (2008), Yu et al. (2007), and Zhou and Lai (2010).

3.3 Model estimation

In this study, the Markov switching model is estimated by applying the maximum likelihood method. Consider the following regime switching model.

$$y_t = \mu_{S_t} + \epsilon_t$$
$$\epsilon_t \sim N(0, \delta_{S_t}^2) \tag{3.12}$$
$$S_t = 1,2$$

The log likelihood of the above model is given by:

$$L(\theta) = \sum_{t=1}^{T} \log\left(\frac{1}{\sqrt{2\pi\sigma_{S_t}^2}} \exp\left(1\frac{y_t - \mu_{S_t}}{2\sigma_{S_t}^2}\right)\right) \tag{3.13}$$

In this model, in order to directly estimate the MS model using the maximum likelihood method, all the states need to be known and the values of S_t are available. So, what we need to do is maximize Equation 3.13, which contains parameters $\mu_1, \mu_1, \delta_1^2, \delta_2^2$. However, as mentioned above, the states of the world are unknown in the Markov switching model. Fortunately, changing the notation for the likelihood function is available for estimating the MS model where the states are unknown.

Considering $f(y_t \mid s_t = j, \theta)$ as the likelihood function for state j conditional on a set of parameters θ, then the full log likelihood function of the model is given by:

$$L(\theta) = \sum_{t=1}^{T} \log f(y_t \mid \theta) = \sum_{t=1}^{T} \log \sum_{j=1}^{2} (f(y_t \mid s_t = j, \theta) P(s_t = j \mid \psi_t)) \tag{3.14}$$

This is just a weighted average of the likelihood function which contains every state of the world, where the weights are given by the state's probabilities. Only if these probabilities are known, can we apply Equation 3.14 directly. But according to the main idea of Hamilton's filter, based on the available information in each state, we can calculate the filtered probabilities, which serve the likelihood Equation 3.14. So far, we have introduced the whole framework of the algorithm, which will be applied to estimate $P(S_t = j)$ in our studies in the following.

ψ_{t-1} is defined as the matrix of available information at time $t - 1$ and there are two states.

Step 1: Set an initial guess for the starting probability of each state $P(S_0 = j)$ for $j = 1,2$. For example, we set $P(S_0 = j) = 0.5$ for $j = 1,2$.

Step 2: Set $t = 1$ and compute the probabilities of each state given information up to time $t - 1$:

$$P(s_t = j \mid \psi_{t-1}) = \sum_{i=1}^{2} p_{ji}(P(s_{t-1} = i \mid \psi_{t-1})) \tag{3.15}$$

Step 3: Update the probability of each state with the new information from time t. Then, use the parameters of the model in each state, $\mu_1, \mu_1, \delta_1^2, \delta_2^2, p_{11}, p_{22}$, to calculate of the likelihood function in each state $f(y_t \mid s_t = j, \psi_{t-1})$ for time t. After that, we need to use the following formula to update the probability of each state given the new information:

$$P(s_t = j \mid \psi_t) = \frac{f(y_t \mid s_t = j, \psi_{t-1})P(s_t = j \mid \psi_{t-1})}{\sum_{j=1}^{2} f(y_t \mid s_t = j, \psi_{t-1})P(s_t = j \mid \psi_{t-1})} \tag{3.16}$$

Step 4: Set $t = t + 1$ and repeat Steps 2 and 3 until $t = T$, until all observations in the sample are reached. In the meantime, a set of filtered probabilities for each state from $t = 1...T$ should be provided. The previous iteration algorithm provides the probabilities that one needs for computing the log likelihood of the model as a function of the set of parameters:

$$L(\theta) = \sum_{t=1}^{T} \log f(y_t \mid \theta) = \sum_{t=1}^{T} \log \sum_{j=1}^{2} (f(y_t \mid s_t = j, \theta)P(s_t = j \mid \psi_t)) \tag{3.17}$$

Through finding the set of parameters to maximize Equation 3.17, we finish the estimation of the model. During the process of estimating the regime switching model, more attention should be paid to the values of parameters in the transition matrix, which must be between zero and one and add up to one in each column of the transition matrix P. For $k = 2$ we can apply a numerical transformation for p_{11} and p_{22} and set $p_{21} = 1 - p_{11}$ and $p_{12} = 1 - p_{22}$ to implement these conditions.

3.4 Empirical analysis

In this section, the weekly data of the RMB exchange rate of CNY are used, from 24 August 2010 to 26 September 2016. This produces a total of 312 observed data series from Bloomberg. Figure 3.1 presents the exchange rate return series of CNY and CNH.

Most researchers in the area of financial economics choose to model the log return of the financial time series. This study also uses the log

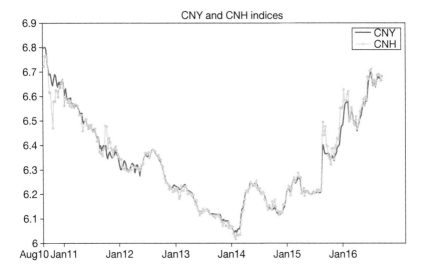

Figure 3.1 CNY and CNH series.

return by taking the natural logarithm of the first difference of the current exchange rate and the previous exchange rate.

Figure 3.2 plots the explained variable, conditional standard deviation, and smoothed states of probabilities for the MS model with CNY series returns. Figure 3.3 plots the explained variable, conditional standard deviation, and smoothed states of probabilities for the EMD-MS model with CNY series returns. In the following, we interpret the empirical results for each model.

For the MS model, Figure 3.3 shows that the mean value of State 1 is negative which implies a low market pressure, which denotes appreciation of currency. On the other hand, State 2 has positive mean value, indicating a high market pressure, which denotes depreciation of currency. Also, the variance of State 2 is bigger than the variance of State 1, which indicates the volatility of State 2 is higher than State 1. From the perspective of a crisis happening, higher volatility implies a higher possibility of currency crisis. Therefore, we can interpret State 1 as a tranquil state and State 2 as a crisis state. In other words, the system is under tranquil periods when State 1 prevails, and under crisis periods when State 2 prevails.

In Table 3.1, when we look at the transition probabilities, both states are very persistent since their self-transition probabilities are both high and close to unit to some extent. Moreover, the tranquil state is more persistent than the crisis state because P_{11} is bigger than P_{22}. On the other

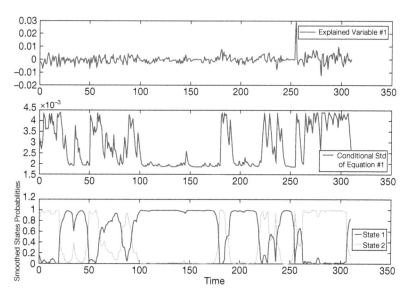

Figure 3.2 Results of MS model estimation.

Table 3.1 MS model estimation for CNY.

State	1	2
Value	−0.0005	0.0006
	(0.0002)	(0.0004)
Variance	0.000003	0.000021
	0.0000	0.0000
Transition Probabilities	0.9519	0.0789
	0.0481	0.9211

side, it is easier for the markets to switch to a tranquil state from a crisis state since P_{12} is larger than P_{21}.

In Figure 3.2, we find that the smoothed probabilities of the crisis state are over 50 percent between September 2010, September 2011, and August 2015, which means the model is sending warning signals to the market for the coming or possible currency crisis. In reality, the CNY series experienced severe depreciation during this time period. Therefore, this evidence shows that the Markov switching model can accomplish the task of identifying a currency crisis.

The estimation results for EMD-MS model are shown in Table 3.2 and Figure 3.3. The results are comparably similar with MS model. According to the two figures of smoothed probabilities, we can clearly find that the EMD-MS model detects more crisis periods than the MS model, which means the EMD-MS model is more sensitive to a currency crisis.

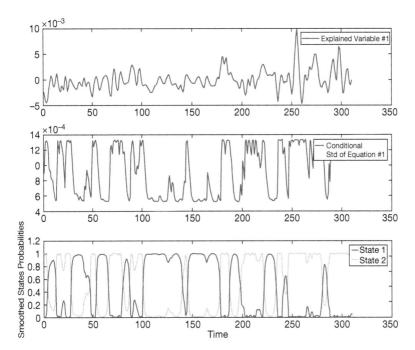

Figure 3.3 Results of EMD-MS model estimation.

Table 3.2 EMD-MS model estimation for CNY.

State	1	2
Value	−0.0001	0.0001
	(0.0000)	(0.0001)
Variance	0.000000	0.000002
	0.0000	0.0000
Transition Probabilities	0.9158	0.0735
	0.0842	0.9265

3.5 Conclusion

This chapter focuses on studying the ability of the Markov switching model to identify and predict a CNY currency crisis. We can apply the Markov switching model to display how the foreign exchange markets switch states before a currency crisis hits. Apart from the volatility of the market pressure index, the mean value is also considered in our Markov switching model. We also find that the main determination of each state is volatility rather than the mean value. With the approach of a currency crisis, our Markov switching model produces a high probability of vulnerability and volatility. Based on the empirical results provided in Table 3.2, we can say that most currency crises could be identified and predicted by the Markov switching model. Thus, identifying a currency crisis endogenously – that is, without knowing the date of currency – could be accomplished by applying the Markov switching model.

In addition, during the process of identifying a CNY currency crisis, we find that the empirical results of the hybrid EMD-MS model are similar to that of the traditional MS model. Nevertheless, compared with the MS model, the EMD-MS model is more sensitive to a currency crisis. In short, the EMD-MS model and traditional MS model have their own advantages in detecting and predicting currency crisis events, and either model can be selected as a currency crisis warning system for the CNY.

4 Forecasting the renminbi exchange rate with an EMD-based neural network

4.1 Introduction

In recent years, China has witnessed sustained and rapid economic growth. According to an IMF report in 2014, for the first time in decades China has surpassed the United States as the largest economy (on a purchasing power parity basis) in the world.[1] Thus, the renminbi (RMB), China's official currency, has attracted global attention from policymakers, investment institutions, and entrepreneurs. According to the Society of Worldwide Interbank Financial Telecommunication (SWIFT) data, in August 2015, the RMB surpassed the Japanese yen to become one of the top four world payment currencies. However, compared with the top three payment currencies, including the US dollar (44.89 percent), euro (27.2 percent), and British pound (8.5 percent), the RMB accounted for only 2.8 percent of the total global payment. On 1 October 2016, the RMB has been included among the IMF's Special Drawing Rights (SDR) as a fifth currency, along with the US dollar, the euro, the Japanese yen, and the British pound. And during the new valuation period, the new currency amounts will determine the value of the SDR (International Monetary Fund, 2016). The RMB has a weighting of 10.92 percent in the new SDR basket, while the respective weighting of other currencies in the basket are 41.73 percent for the US dollar, 30.93 percent for the euro, 8.33 percent for the Japanese yen, and 8.09 percent for the British pound, according to the IMF.

With the continuing development of RMB internationalization, more policymakers, individual investors, financial institutions, and multinational corporations are participating in RMB currency trading. Establishing the RMB offshore center in Hong Kong in 2004 was the first step in the process of RMB internationalization. In December 2008, Chinese Premier Wen Jiabao announced a pilot program for the cross-border trade settlement of the RMB with Hong Kong.

Then the RMB became officially deliverable in Hong Kong on 19 July 2010, with a joint announcement from the People's Bank of China (PBOC) and the Hong Kong Monetary Authority (HKMA). Thus, the market for the CNH had officially commenced. Some studies, including Henning (2012), Subramanian and Kessler (2014), Fratzscher and Mehl (2014), and Shu et al. (2015) have shown that regional currencies were impacted by RMB movements.

Because of the importance of the RMB, establishing an effective RMB forecasting model and providing a feasible application for designing trading strategies are indispensable, which is also the purpose of this chapter. We will take into account two kinds of current exchange rates for the US dollar (USD) to the RMB. At present, China's capital account is not yet fully open. Although there is only one Chinese currency, the onshore exchange market in mainland China is partly separated from the offshore exchange market centered in Hong Kong. The CNY is the RMB traded onshore, while the CNH is the RMB traded offshore. Obviously, due to changes in financial markets, the two RMB exchange markets usually respond differently, which means that the CNY and CNH trade at different exchange rates. Craig et al. (2013) and Funke et al. (2015) have studied the CNY–CNH pricing differentials in detail.

Many linear models – for example, the autoregressive integrated moving average (ARIMA) model – have been applied to model financial time series in foreign exchange and stock markets. However, previous studies show that the asset price series are nonlinear, and rarely pure linear, combinations in the real-world financial market (Zhang, et al., 1998; Zhang, 2001; Khashei et al., 2009). Thus, in order to research the forecasting ability of the financial time series, many artificial intelligence nonlinear models came into being including artificial neural networks (ANN), support vector regression (SVR), and genetic programming (GP). Forecasting the foreign exchange rate with ANN was reviewed in detail by Yu et al. (2010); they also introduced SVR and GP. In this chapter, we will focus on applying ANN to forecast the RMB exchange rate with different forecasting horizons of 1, 5, 10, 20 and 30 days. However, a study conducted by Huang et al. (2003) shows that when the forecasting period is within five days, the ANN performs better than the random walk; for the longer horizon, the situation is exactly the opposite. Also, multilayer perceptrons (MLP), a class of feed-forward artificial neural network model, will be applied in our study. A hybrid model – empirical mode decomposition (EMD), which helps improve forecasting performance – is also included in our empirical studies.

Huang et al. (1998) were the first to propose empirical mode decomposition, which consists of a finite and often small number of intrinsic mode functions (IMFs) and one residual. In our study, to simplify the forecasting task into simpler subtasks, we will apply empirical mode decomposition to decompose the original time series data into components. At present, empirical mode decomposition has been widely used in different fields. For example, the EMD-based neural network model conducted by Yu et al. (2008) is used to forecast crude oil prices; tourism demand was also forecasted by the combination of EMD and ANN, researched by Chen et al. (2011). Also, the hybrid forecasting model proposed by Lin et al. (2012), which combined EMD and SVR, was used to forecast foreign exchange rates. In our empirical experiment, we will apply EMD to divide the original CNY or CNH price series, which are nonlinear and nonstationary, into several independent subseries. Then, it becomes easier to forecast part or all of the IMFs and one residual.

Similar to our study, the study by Yu et al. (2008) have proposed the hybrid forecasting model that combines MLP and EMD. Nevertheless, the difference is that the impact of IMFs that have different levels of frequency will be examined further in this study. To be specific, if the forecasting horizon is longer, the higher frequency IMFs might be considered as noise components. Thus, we propose two hybrid models, EMD-MLP and EMD-MLP*, which adjust the original time series data by deducting higher-frequency IMFs and calculate the forecast for the previous day by using the MLP. The principle of "divide and conquer" is applied in the EMD-MLP* model, which is used to establish the novel forecasting methodology, where some or all IMFs and one residual are used. Based on the empirical results in our study, whether it is 1, 5, 10, 20, or 30 days of the forecasting horizons, both EMD-MLP and EMD-MLP* are superior to the pure MLP model. In addition, the trading strategies are tested in our empirical experiment. Trading performance shows that, even given a 0.3 percent transaction cost in each trade, the trading strategy based on EMD-MLP has an average annual profit of more than 10 percent.

The rest of the chapter is organized as follows. Section 4.2 introduces ANN and EMD, including their forecasting process and model notations of three kinds of forecasting models. The selected models, along with the abovementioned CNY and CNH that are used to test the effectiveness of the proposed methodology, are applied in the trading strategies in Section 4.3. Section 4.4 concludes the chapter.

4.2 Methodology

4.2.1 Artificial neural network (ANN)

The artificial neural network (ANN) is a computational model widely used in computer science and other research disciplines. It is based on a large collection of simple neural units and inspired by biological neural networks. This study considers the multilayer perceptron (MLP), which is based on the error back-propagation algorithm. The underlying network structure of an MLP, composed by weights (synapses) and nodes (neurons), is a directed graph. For example, as shown in Figure 4.1, a simple MLP structure has three input nodes (X1, X2, and X3), one hidden layer composed of four hidden nodes, and one output node (Y). The nodes, organized hierarchically, are usually fully connected by weights, where the weights indicate the effects of the corresponding nodes. In each node of the hidden and output layers, first the integration function (also called the *summation function*) combines all incoming signals. Then the activation function (also called the transfer function) transforms the output of the node.

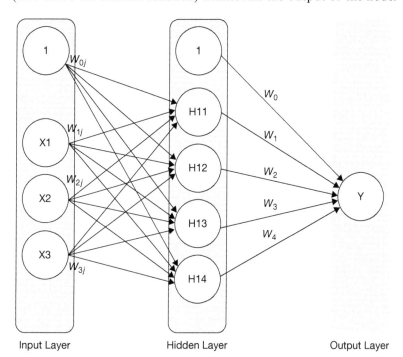

Figure 4.1 An artificial neural network structure.

Generally, because of the converging restriction, the number of hidden layers is less than three. Any continuous function can be approximated well by a three-layer feed-forward neural network with a sufficient amount of hidden layer neurons (Hornik, Stinchcombe, & White, 1989; White, 1990).

Figure 4.1 shows an artificial neural network structure with three input neurons (X1, X2, and X3), one hidden layer consisting of four hidden neurons (H11, H12, H13, and H14), and one output neuron (Y).

In practice, after being fitted by the training data, the MLP model applies the testing data from an out-of-sample dataset to test the forecasting performance. Under the supervised learning algorithms, the approach of minimizing the forecasting error function can be used to adjust the parameters, which are weights and node intercepts. Therefore, an MLP with an input layer with n nodes, one hidden layer consisting of J hidden nodes, and an output layer with one output node calculates the following function:

$$o(x) = f(w_0 + \sum_{j=1}^{J} w_j \cdot f(w_{0j} + \sum_{i=1}^{n} w_{ij}x_i))$$

$$= f(w_0 + \sum_{j=1}^{J} w_j \cdot f(w_{0j} + w_j^T x)), \tag{4.1}$$

where $x = (x_1, \ldots, x_n)$ is the vector of all input variables, w_0 is the intercept of the output node, w_{0j} is the intercept of the jth hidden node, w_j denotes the weight corresponding to the node starting at the jth hidden node to the output node, and w_{ij} denotes the weight corresponding to the node starting at ith input node to the jth hidden node. Thus, all hidden and output nodes calculate the function $f(g(z))$. In this function, $g(\cdot)$, defined as $g(z) = w_0 + w'z$, denotes the integration function; and $f(\cdot)$, usually as a bounded, nondecreasing, nonlinear, and differentiable function, denotes the activation function.

If inputs x and the current weights, initialized with random values from a standard normal distribution, are given, the MLP will produce an output $o(x)$. Then an error function is denied. Consider the mean squared error (MSE) in the following:

$$E = \frac{1}{N} \sum_{h=1}^{N} (o_h(x) - y_h)^2 \tag{4.2}$$

where N is the number of data samples and y_h is the observed output. During the iterative training process, according to the resilient back propagation algorithm, all weights need to be adapted by repeating the above steps until a pre-specified criterion is fulfilled, where the algorithm is explained in detail by Rojas (2013). To find a local minimum of the error function, the weights are modified in the opposite direction of partial derivatives by the resilient back-propagation algorithm. According to Riedmiller and Braun (1993), the weights are adjusted by the following rule:

$$w_k^{(t+1)} = w_k^t - \eta_k^{(t)} \cdot \text{sign}\left(\frac{\partial E^{(t)}}{\partial w_k^{(t)}}\right), \tag{4.3}$$

where t and k index the iteration steps and the weights, respectively. Compared with the fixed learning rate of the traditional back-propagation algorithm, in the case where the corresponding partial derivative remains the same symbol, speeding up convergence will increase the learning rate $\eta_k^{(t)}$ in the above equation; otherwise, it will be decreased. Furthermore, the neuralnet package of R software (version number 1.33), introduced in Günther and Fritsch (2010), is applied in the MLP.

4.2.2 Empirical mode decomposition (EMD)

Empirical mode decomposition (EMD), an adaptive time series decomposition technique first proposed by Huang et al. (1998), will be further considered in this chapter. Nonlinear and nonstationary time series data can be decomposed into several intrinsic mode functions (IMFs) and remaining residues by applying the EMD which introduces the Hilbert–Huang transform (HHT). The first condition is usually adopted in other decomposition techniques, but the second condition allows the IMFs to be asymmetrically oscillatory. Generally, these IMFs should satisfy the following two conditions: first, the number of extrema must be equal to zero crossings, or differ by not more than one. Second, the mean value of the envelopes, including both upper and lower ones defined by local maxima and minima, must be zero at all points. Often, decomposition techniques adopted the first condition while the second condition is looser, in which asymmetric oscillation is allowed.

A sifting process proposed by Huang et al. (1998) can be applied to decompose the time series data $x(t)$, $t = 1, 2, \ldots, T$. First, find out all local minima and local maxima of $x(t)$, and then connect all local extrema with a spline line to define the upper and lower envelopes. Next, calculate the mean value $m_1^1(t)$ from the upper and lower envelopes at all points of the envelope. Then the first IMF of $x(t)$ is:

$$h_1^1(t) = x(t) - m_1^1(t) \tag{4.4}$$

If $h_1^1(t)$ does not satisfy the above two conditions, then $h_1^1(t)$ will be regarded as a new data series and repeated in Procedure 4. Thus, we calculate

$$h_2^1(t) = h_1^1(t) - m_2^1(t) \tag{4.5}$$

In Equation 4.5, $m_2^1(t)$ is the mean value of the upper and lower envelopes of $h_1^1(t)$. Repeat the same procedure until meeting both conditions, then we get the first IMF component of $x(t)$, $c_1(t)$.

Through repeating the same procedure until satisfying the above conditions,[2] the first IMF component of $x(t)$, $c_1(t)$ will be obtained:

$$c_1(t) = h_q^1(t) \tag{4.6}$$

And then, another series $r_1(t) = x(t) - c_1(t)$, containing all information except $c_1(t)$, is defined. Huang et al. (2003) suggest a sifting stop criterion to generate all IMFs by the same sifting procedure until $r_n(t)$ becomes a monotonic function or cannot extract more IMFs. A sifting stop criterion, proposed by Huang et al. (2003), is applied to generate all IMFs. By repeating the same sifting procedure, $r_n(t)$ finally will become a monotonic function or cannot extract more IMFs. Therefore, the time series $x(t)$ can be expressed as:

$$x(t) = \sum_{i=1}^{n} c_i(t) + r_n(t) \tag{4.7}$$

where n is the amount of IMFs and $r_n(t)$ is the final residue denoting the central tendency of data series $x(t)$. Besides, these IMFs are nearly orthogonal to each other and all have means of nearly zero. Based on the above properties, by forecasting all decompositions and summarizing these estimations, it is possible to produce the prediction of $x(t)$.

Furthermore, EMD is easy to implement in many software programs. In this chapter, the decomposition work is completed by applying the

EMD package in R software (version number 1.5.7). Compared with the traditional wavelet decomposition, the EMD does not need to determine a filter base function before decomposition. Thus, the EMD, a very effective decomposition tool, could decompose time series data into several nearly independent IMF components and one residual.

4.2.3 Overall forecasting process and model notations

Given a time series p_t, $t = 1, 2, \ldots, T$, where $\hat{p}_{t+l}$ is defined as the l-day ahead prediction. For instance, $l = 2$ denotes a two-day-ahead prediction and $l = 5$ represents a five-day-ahead prediction. Actually, in Equation 4.1, the MLP model performs nonlinear functional mapping from past observations to the future price value. In this study, the input variables (past observations) include p_{t-60}, p_{t-20}, p_{t-10}, and p_{t-5} to p_{t-1}, which represent the past price levels of one season, one month, two weeks, and a single week, respectively. Then, the output is the l-day-ahead prediction. Thus, the equation can be expressed as:

$$\hat{p}_{t+l} = \varphi(p_{t-1}, \ldots, p_{t-5}, p_{t-10}, p_{t-20}, p_{t-60}, w) + \xi_t \qquad (4.8)$$

where $\varphi(\cdot)$ is a function which is determined by neural network train-ing, w is a weight vector of all parameters of MLP, and ξ_t is a noise. According to the studies from Yu et al. (2005, 2010), the MLP model is equivalent to a nonlinear autoregressive model.

This study also includes three kinds of forecasting models. One of the forecasting models is the pure MLP model, which has two differ-ent states. If the pure MLP model with one hidden layer, MLP(J_1), is defined as the notation of this model. And the pure MLP model with two hidden layers, MLP(J_1; J_2), is defined as the notation of this model. In order to decompose the original time series, another two models, the EMD-MLP model and the EMD-MLP* model are used in the EMD. For the EMD-MLP model, first we use it to deduct some volatile IMFs in the original data series and generate a new one, where some volatile IMF components cause certain noise effects. For instance, considering 30-day-ahead predictions, the first part of IMF is usually unnecessary and may diminish the effectiveness of the forecast. As shown in Figure 4.2, the first IMF is subtracted in the procedure of the EMD(-1)-MLP model. Then, under the technology of the MLP model, we use the new data series to calculate the final prediction.

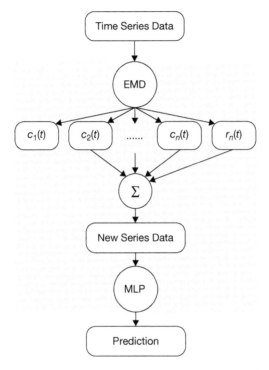

Figure 4.2 An example of the EMD(-1)-MLP model.

We decompose a time series dataset by EMD and generate n IMF components, $c_1(t), c_1(t), ..., c_1(t)$, and one residue $r_n(t)$. We sum all decompositions except $c_1(t)$ to produce a new time series dataset. Then the MLP is applied to compute the prediction.

The EMD-MLP* model, inspired by the work of Yu et al. (2008) is the third kind of model. This EMD-based neural network ensemble forecasting model usually consists of the following four steps:

1 Decompose the original time series into IMF components and one residual component by applying EMD.
2 Determine the amount of IMF components, which rely on the length of the forecasting period.
3 Use MLP to model IMF components and the residual component, and then make the corresponding prediction.
4 Finally, generate the final prediction result for the original time series by adding all prediction results to one value.

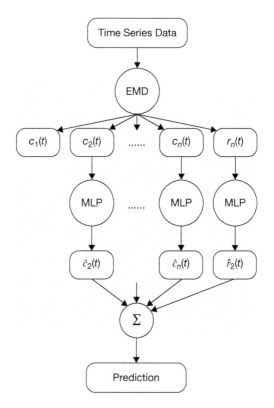

Figure 4.3 An example of the EMD(-1)-MLP* model

As shown in Figure 4.3, under the technology of EMD, time series data is decomposed into n IMF components, $c_1(t)$, $c_2(t)$,..., $c_n(t)$ and one residue $r_n(t)$. Apart from $c_1(t)$, each of the decompositions is predicted and summed up as the final prediction for the original time series.

We decompose a time series data by the EMD and generate n IMF components, $c_1(t), c_2(t),...,c_n(t)$ and one residue $r_n(t)$. Besides $c_1(t)$, we forecast each decomposition and then sum them as the prediction.

4.3 Empirical experiments

4.3.1 Data

This chapter considers two kinds of currency exchange rates of USD to RMB. As mentioned in Section 4.1, CNY refers to the RMB traded onshore – that is, in mainland China. When the RMB is traded offshore, it is referred to as CNH. We download both CNY and CNH data from Bloomberg, where the CNY date ranges from 2 January 2006 to 21 December 2015 with a total of 2,584 observations. Because the off-shore market was officially established on 19 July 2010, the period of CNH dates range from 3 January 2011 to 21 December 2015 with a total of 1,304 observations. In order to train the neural network models, we assign two-thirds of the observations as the training dataset randomly and the rest as the testing dataset.

As introduced in Section 2.2, both the CNY and CNH price time series are decomposed into several independent IMFs and one residual component by the EMD technique. Figures 4.4 and 4.5 provide the decomposed results of the CNY and CNH time series. Because of different lengths of sample periods, the raw data series and decompositions of the CNY and CNH time series seem different when comparing the two figures.

The EMD decompositions from 2006 to 2015 include the raw data series, six IMFs, and one residual.

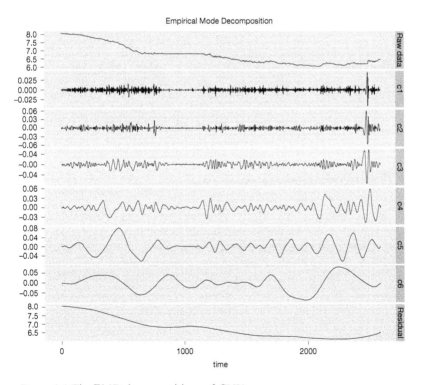

Figure 4.4 The EMD decompositions of CNY.

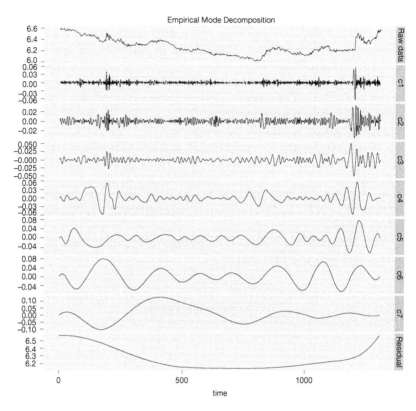

Figure 4.5 The EMD decompositions of CNH.

The EMD decompositions of CNH from 2011 to 2015 include the raw data series, seven IMFs, and one residual.

By analyzing the two figures in detail, we can find some similar features. First, it is obvious to find that the residual components of CNY and CNH data have the same trend during the data period of 2011 to 2015. At first the residual components remain at about 6.5, then decline to 6.2, and finally come back to 6.5. Also, the swing period of the high-frequency IMFs is shorter. Compared to low frequency, the mean of the absolute values of the high-frequency IMFs is also smaller. For instance, the absolute value of c_1, c_3, and c_5 are 0.00298, 0.00596, and 0.02002 in the CNY series.

In fact, when the forecasting period is long, high-frequency IMFs may reduce predicted accuracy; that is, there is no need to include all high-frequency IMFs in our empirical study. Therefore, we removed the high-frequency IMFs to get the denoised time series in the model EMD-MLP and EMD-MLP*. It is worth mentioning that not only are all the decompositions used to forecast the exchange rate, but also part of the decompositions except the high-frequency IMFs in the model EMD-MLP*.

4.3.2 Experimental results

Consider the two main criteria in the empirical experiments: the mean squared error (MSE) and the directional statistic (D_{stat}). Both are introduced to evaluate level prediction and directional forecasting, respectively. Thus, the MSE is defined as:

$$MSE = \frac{1}{N_t} \sum_{s \in \Psi} (\hat{p}_{s+l} - p_{s+l})^2 \tag{4.9}$$

where Ψ refers to the test dataset containing N_t observations, $\hat{p}_{s+l}$ is the l-day-ahead prediction, and p_{s+l} is the actual value. Clearly, the MSE is one of the most important criteria for measuring the validity of one forecasting model, but from the business perspective, improving the accuracy of directional predictions can support decision making, so as to generate greater profit.

The MSE is one of the most important criteria, widely used to measure the validity of one forecasting model. In terms of business perspective, for better decision making and getting more profits, we need to improve the accuracy of directional predictions. Based on Yu et al. (2005, 2008), we introduce D_{stat} to examine the ability of predicting movement direction. D_{stat} is defined by:

$$D_{stat} = \frac{1}{N_t} \sum_{s \in \Psi} a_s \times 100\% \tag{4.10}$$

where $a_s = 1$ if $(\hat{p}_{s+l} - p_s)(p_{s+l} - p_s) \geq 0$, and $a_s = 0$ otherwise.

The forecasting performances of MSE for the MLP, EMD-MLP, and EMD-MLP* models are provided in Table 4.1, where the MSE is reported as the percentage for l-day-ahead predictions and $l = 1, 5, 10, 20,$ and 30.

For each prediction period, the minimum MSE is designated in bold font. The empirical results of MLP are shown in Panel A of Table 4.1.

Table 4.1 The MSE comparisons for different models.

	1-day	5-day	10-day	20-day	30-day
Panel A: MLP model					
MLP(3)	0.0081	0.0296	0.0693	0.1246	0.1909
MLP(5)	0.0072	0.0289	0.0683	0.1328	0.1855
MLP(5,3)	0.0100	0.0319	0.0670	0.1221	0.1539
MLP(6,4)	0.0132	0.0303	0.0661	0.1218	0.1768
Panel B: EMD-MLP model					
EMD(-1)-MLP(3)	0.0057	0.0310	0.0740	0.1278	0.1975
EMD(-1)-MLP(5,3)	0.0030	0.0292	0.0685	0.1301	0.1703
EMD(-2)-MLP(3)	0.0066	0.0151	0.0542	0.1242	0.1814
EMD(-2)-MLP(5,3)	0.0075	0.0148	0.0491	0.1317	0.1607
EMD(-3)-MLP(3)	0.0141	0.0138	0.0232	0.0725	0.1405
EMD(-3)-MLP(5,3)	0.0138	0.0144	0.0214	0.0738	0.1178
Panel C: EMD-MLP* model					
EMD(0)-MLP(3)*	0.0035	0.0081	0.0160	0.0285	0.0422
EMD(0)-MLP(5,3)*	0.0038	0.0116	0.0148	**0.0254**	0.0364
EMD(-1)-MLP(3)*	0.0029	**0.0074**	0.0148	0.0286	0.0406
EMD(-1)-MLP(5,3)*	**0.0025**	0.0082	**0.0119**	0.0256	**0.0334**
EMD(-2)-MLP(3)*	0.0063	0.0079	0.0172	0.0269	0.0387
EMD(-2)-MLP(5,3)*	0.0069	0.0098	0.0142	0.0274	0.0335

As the forecasting period increases, the value of MSE becomes larger, meaning that for a longer forecasting period, forecasting accuracy reduces. However, for more complicated MLP models with two hidden layers, empirical results do not provide better forecasting accuracy, and are even worse for one-day-ahead predictions.

Panel B of Table 4.1 displays the empirical results of EMD-MLP. The highest frequency IMF c_1, treated as noise by EMD(-1)-MLP, is removed from the original time series. Then, the MLP model is applied to forecast the exchange rate. However, experimental results of EMD(-1)-MLP show that the MSE of one-day-ahead forecasting declines significantly and the improvement of five-day-ahead forecasting is limited. Empirical results show that EMD(-2)-MLP models, which treat the two highest-frequency IMF series as noise and remove them, have better performance than EMD(-1)-MLP models in the five-day-ahead forecasting experiment. Similarly, the EMD(-3)-MLP models have better performance in the ten-day-ahead forecasting experiment. The empirical results of EMD-MLP* models are discussed in Panel C of Table 4.1. Compared to MLP and EMD-MLP, the calculation process of EMD(-1)-MLP* is more complex. However, according to the criteria of MSE, the forecasting performance of EMD(-1)-MLP* is much better. To be more specific, EMD(-1)-MLP* models, which deduct all the high-frequency IMF series, always have better performance in predictions of different periods.

Empirical results of evaluating the forecasting performance of three models with D_{stat} are provided in Table 4.2, which are similar to the results of MSE criteria. As shown in Panel C of Table 4.2, when we use EMD(-2)-MLP(5,3)* to forecast the direction of the CNY series in the ten-day-ahead forecasting experiment, the hitting rate can be up to 86.63%.

As mentioned in the empirical results of MSE, the calculation process of EMD-MLP* models is relatively more complex. However, compared to the other two models, the forecasting performance of EMD-MLP* models is much better. EMD(-1)-MLP* models, which deduct the highest frequency IMF treated as noise, have better forecasting performance based on both MSE and D_{stat} criteria.

Table 4.1 above considers the CNY from 2 January 2006 to 21 December 2015 with a total of 2,584 observations. This table compares the forecasting performance, in terms of the MSE, for the MLP, EMD-MLP, and EMD-MLP* models. We report the MSE as a percentage for *l*-day-ahead predictions where $l = 1, 5, 10, 20,$ and 30. For each length of prediction, we mark the minimum MSE as bold.

Table 4.2 considers the CNY from 2 January 2006 to 21 December 2015 with a total of 2,584 observations. This table compares the forecasting performance, in terms of D_{stat}, for the MLP, EMD-MLP, and EMD-MLP* models. We report D_{stat} as a percentage for *l*-day-ahead predictions where $l = 1, 5, 10, 20,$ and 30. For each length of prediction, we mark the maximum D_{stat} as bold.

Apart from the empirical study of MSE and D_{stat}, we also consider the dataset of the CNY and CNH series from 2011 to 2015, which are divided into the training set and testing set. From the empirical results

Table 4.2 The D_{stat} comparisons for different models.

	1-day	*5-day*	*10-day*	*20-day*	*30-day*
Panel A: MLP model					
MLP(3)	51.74	53.49	63.49	69.65	70.72
MLP(5)	51.98	55.17	62.17	68.44	71.08
MLP(5,3)	50.18	54.93	65.78	69.29	73.39
MLP(6,4)	48.98	55.41	62.65	69.89	71.20
Panel B: EMD-MLP model					
EMD(-1)-MLP(3)	62.30	56.49	63.73	69.65	70.11
EMD(-1)-MLP(5,3)	**74.19**	57.33	67.71	69.29	71.45
EMD(-2)-MLP(3)	65.55	70.31	68.80	71.10	70.35
EMD(-2)-MLP(5,3)	62.06	69.95	70.60	70.98	73.39
EMD(-3)-MLP(3)	57.74	74.04	78.67	75.33	74.48
EMD(-3)-MLP(5,3)	57.98	74.52	80.60	74.37	74.48
Panel C: EMD-MLP* model					
EMD(0)-MLP(3)*	68.91	79.57	77.83	**82.35**	86.63
EMD(0)-MLP(5,3)*	69.27	74.28	78.07	82.10	86.03
EMD(-1)-MLP(3)*	71.07	80.77	77.95	82.10	84.45
EMD(-1)-MLP(5,3)*	72.63	**81.49**	**84.46**	81.86	86.51
EMD(-2)-MLP(3)*	63.63	79.33	77.47	81.86	85.54
EMD(-2)-MLP(5,3)*	63.63	76.56	80.84	81.98	**86.63**

in Table 4.1 and Table 4.2, we can find that only EMD-MLP models are applied to do forecasting, and MLP models are not considered. Tables 4.3 and 4.4 provide the statistical results of MSE and D_{stat}, respectively.

According to both MSE and D_{stat} criteria, experimental results show that EMD-MLP* models have better performance than EMD-MLP models. Analyzing the MSE comparisons for CNY and CNH in Table 4.3, it is clear that the MSE of CNH is greater than that of CNY

Table 4.3 The MSE comparisons for CNY and CNH.

	1-day	5-day	10-day	20-day	30-day
Panel A: CNY					
EMD(-1)-MLP(5,3)	0.0036	0.0196	0.0796	0.1471	0.1644
EMD(-2)-MLP(5,3)	0.0048	0.0120	0.0605	0.0976	0.1431
EMD(-3)-MLP(5,3)	0.0093	0.0108	0.0176	0.0736	0.1252
EMD(0)-MLP(3)*	0.0033	0.0062	0.0100	0.0214	0.0294
EMD(0)-MLP(5,3)*	0.0032	0.0061	0.0100	0.0190	0.0240
EMD(-1)-MLP(3)*	0.0023	0.0059	0.0103	0.0241	0.0297
EMD(-1)-MLP(5,3)*	0.0025	0.0070	0.0088	0.0176	0.0268
EMD(-2)-MLP(3)*	0.0042	0.0067	0.0113	0.0186	0.0268
EMD(-2)-MLP(5,3)*	0.0045	0.0071	0.0122	0.0172	0.0236
Panel B: CNH					
EMD(-1)-MLP(5,3)	0.0075	0.0420	0.0991	0.2076	0.3104
EMD(-2)-MLP(5,3)	0.0076	0.0177	0.0558	0.1703	0.3058
EMD(-3)-MLP(5,3)	0.0150	0.0154	0.0359	0.1084	0.2634
EMD(0)-MLP(3)*	0.0037	0.0131	0.0208	0.0402	0.0531
EMD(0)-MLP(5,3)*	0.0044	0.0116	0.0230	0.0415	0.0493
EMD(-1)-MLP(3)*	0.0045	0.0116	0.0231	0.0360	0.0574
EMD(-1)-MLP(5,3)*	0.0044	0.0122	0.0221	0.0323	0.0463
EMD(-2)-MLP(3)*	0.0069	0.0105	0.0205	0.0382	0.0537
EMD(-2)-MLP(5,3)*	0.0070	0.0120	0.0204	0.0381	0.0486

on average during any forecasting period, because the original volatility of the CNH series is greater than that of the CNY series.

However, with the increase of forecasting periods, the forecasting performance improves in the D_{stat} test part. Based on D_{stat} criteria, there is no dramatic difference between the results of the CNY and CNH series. The value of D_{stat} can be as high as 78 percent in

Table 4.4 The D_{stat} Comparisons for CNY and CNH.

	1-day	5-day	10-day	20-day	30-day
Panel A: CNY					
EMD(-1)-MLP(5,3)	76.85	62.62	62.53	62.41	72.73
EMD(-2)-MLP(5,3)	68.23	75.50	63.28	67.17	68.18
EMD(-3)-MLP(5,3)	62.56	75.74	82.88	76.69	70.20
EMD(0)-MLP(3)*	76.60	78.96	84.37	86.22	85.61
EMD(0)-MLP(5,3)*	78.08	82.18	83.87	89.22	87.63
EMD(-1)-MLP(3)*	75.62	82.67	83.87	86.22	84.60
EMD(-1)-MLP(5,3)*	75.86	83.66	86.10	88.47	85.86
EMD(-2)-MLP(3)*	69.21	81.44	82.88	89.47	84.60
EMD(-2)-MLP(5,3)*	68.97	82.43	83.87	87.22	86.87
Panel B: CNH					
EMD(-1)-MLP(5,3)	66.42	60.88	62.99	65.10	68.08
EMD(-2)-MLP(5,3)	68.61	78.24	68.38	66.34	68.08
EMD(-3)-MLP(5,3)	62.29	79.46	80.64	75.99	76.06
EMD(0)-MLP(3)*	79.81	82.64	84.07	84.65	89.53
EMD(0)-MLP(5,3)*	77.37	81.42	82.84	84.41	90.27
EMD(-1)-MLP(3)*	76.89	80.68	84.56	85.15	85.79
EMD(-1)-MLP(5,3)*	75.18	83.13	84.80	86.14	90.02
EMD(-2)-MLP(3)*	72.26	82.40	84.56	87.62	91.02
EMD(-2)-MLP(5,3)*	72.99	84.60	83.82	84.41	91.02

one-day-ahead forecasting; for over 20-day-ahead forecasting, the hitting accuracy even exceeds 85 percent.

Consider both the CNY and CNH from 3 January 2011 to 21 December 2015 with a total of 1,304 observations in Table 4.3. This table compares the forecasting performance, in terms of the MSE, for several forecasting models. We report the MSE as a percentage for *l*-day-ahead predictions where $l = 1$, 5, 10, 20, and 30. For each length of prediction, we mark the minimum MSE as bold.

Consider both the CNY and CNH from 3 January 2011 to 21 December 2015 with a total of 1,304 observations. This table compares the forecasting performance, in terms of D_{stat}, for several forecasting models. We report D_{stat} as a percentage for l-day-ahead predictions where $l = 1$, 5, 10, 20, and 30 . For each length of prediction, we mark the maximum D_{stat} as bold.

4.3.3 Applying the trading strategy

An application used for designing trading strategy on CNY will be introduced in this section.[3] Based on the empirical results in Table 4.1 and Table 4.2, MSE and D_{stat} criteria, we can construct the best model for l-day-ahead predictions. Based on past exchange rate series, the forecasting model can be trained and then generate l-day-ahead predictions, which can be used to construct trading strategies. Therefore, the trading strategies can be expressed as:

$$\text{Long: if } \hat{p}_{s+l} \geq p_s \times (1+\tau)$$
$$\text{Short: if } \hat{p}_{s+l} < p_s \times (1-\tau) \tag{4.11}$$

where τ is a critical number. Given $\tau = 0$, which means that if l-day-ahead predictions are greater than the present price, we will long the CNY; otherwise, it will be shorted. Therefore, if the price forecasted by the model will rise l days later, then we will long the asset; otherwise, we will short it. For instance, given $\tau = 1\%$, which means that the forecasted price exceeds the present price more than 1 percent, and we will buy the asset; otherwise, we sell it. Considering transaction cost leads to a decline in profits, especially in high-frequency trading, we introduce parameter τ. In order to better evaluate the strategy, transaction costs defined respectively as 0.0%, 0.1%, 0.2%, and 0.3% will be deducted from the original returns.

The empirical results of the above trading strategy are provided in Table 4.5. Based on the empirical results in Tables 4.1 and 4.2, in terms of MSE and D_{stat}, the best performance models with different forecasting periods are shown in Panels A and B, respectively. As shown in the last four columns, we have adjusted annual returns with different transaction costs. It is easy to find that as the value of l increases – that is, the forecasting period becomes longer – the standard deviation will be

Table 4.5 Performance of trading strategy with $\tau=0\%$ based on EMD-MLP.

		N_s	$SD\%$	Return with transaction cost %			
				0.0%	0.1%	0.2%	0.3%
Panel A: Best models (MSE)							
1-day	EMD(-1)-MLP(5,3)*	833	1.46	13.09	-11.91	-36.91	-61.91
5-day	EMD(-1)-MLP(3)*	832	1.53	7.02	2.02	-2.98	-7.98
10-day	EMD(-1)-MLP(5,3)*	830	1.70	6.19	3.69	1.19	-1.31
20-day	EMD(0)-MLP(5,3)*	827	1.76	4.94	3.69	2.44	1.19
30-day	EMD(-1)-MLP(5,3)*	823	1.75	4.52	3.69	2.86	2.02
Panel B: Best models (D_{stat})							
1-day	EMD(-1)-MLP(5,3)	833	1.45	13.27	-11.73	-36.73	-61.73
5-day	EMD(-1)-MLP(5,3)*	832	1.52	7.12	2.12	-2.88	-7.88
10-day	EMD(-1)-MLP(5,3)*	830	1.70	6.19	3.69	1.19	-1.31
20-day	EMD(0)-MLP(3)*	827	1.78	4.88	3.63	2.38	1.13
30-day	EMD(-2)-MLP(5,3)*	823	1.73	4.59	3.76	2.92	2.09

larger. If transaction costs are not considered, then the return decreases with the increasing of the forecasting period *l*. To be more specific, considering a one-day forecasting period experiment, the annual return of the best performance model EMD(-1)-MLP(5,3)* reaches 13.09 percent according to MSE criteria. However, the return declines to 4.52 percent in the forecasting period of 30 days.

On the contrary, if we take transaction costs into account, the return increases with the increasing of forecasting period *l*. Nevertheless, from a short forecasting period perspective, the annual return which is offset by the significant cost of high-frequency trading will drop dramatically. Consider a 0.3-percent trading cost: according to the MSE criteria, the annual return of the best performance model, EMD(-1)-MLP(5,3)*, for 30-day-ahead forecasting is 2.02 percent while the annual returns of the best performance model are as low as -61.91 percent in one-day-ahead forecasting. As for the empirical results shown in the last four columns of Table 4.5, there is no significant difference in the trading strategy results based on best-performance models with MSE and D_{stat} criteria.

For any length of forecasting period, the annual returns with MSE and D_{stat} criteria have similar characteristics. With the increasing of transaction costs for every forecasting period, the annual return decreases.

In terms of MSE and D_{stat}, we select the best models for forecasting l-day models and it is denoted as N_S, shown in Table 4.5. By the trading strategy rule, as in Equation 11 with $\tau = 0$, we generate N_S l-day returns. The fourth column reports the standard deviation of the annualized returns without transaction costs. The last four columns represent the averages of N_S annualized returns with different transaction costs.

Table 4.6 and Table 4.7 display a trading strategy performance based on the best model when $\tau = 0.5\%$ and $\tau = 1\%$, respectively. From the empirical results shown in Tables 4.6 and 4.7, we find that the one-day forecasting case is ignored. The reason for this is the value of the one-day forecasting period is smaller than τ. With the increasing transaction costs in the same forecasting period, the annual return decreases, which is similar to Table 4.5 mentioned above. However, considering the same transaction cost, with the growth of the forecasting period, the annual return decreases, which is the opposite of the case in Table 4.5.

Table 4.6 Performance of trading strategy with $\tau = 0.5\%$ based on EMD-MLP.

				Return with transaction cost %			
		N_s	SD	0.0%	0.1%	0.2%	0.3%
Panel A: Best models (MSE)							
5-day	EMD(-1)-MLP(3)*	37	3.51	34.38	29.38	24.38	19.38
10-day	EMD(-1)-MLP(5,3)*	112	2.80	19.18	16.68	14.18	11.68
20-day	EMD(0)-MLP(5,3)*	229	2.00	11.98	10.73	9.48	8.23
30-day	EMD(-1)-MLP(5,3)*	350	1.74	8.53	7.69	6.86	6.03
Panel B: Best models (D_{stat})							
5-day	EMD(-1)-MLP(5,3)*	41	3.60	31.55	26.55	21.55	16.55
10-day	EMD(-1)-MLP(5,3)*	112	2.80	19.18	16.68	14.18	11.68
20-day	EMD(0)-MLP(3)*	229	2.03	11.90	10.65	9.40	8.15
30-day	EMD(-2)-MLP(5,3)*	364	1.75	8.30	7.47	6.64	5.80

This may be the result of setting $\tau = 0.5\%$ or $\tau = 1\%$; the annual return will not be eroded by trading costs. Consider $\tau = 0.5\%$ in Table 4.6. As shown in Panel A of Table 4.6, the average annual return with different trading costs based on MSE criteria is at least 19.38 percent in a five-day forecasting period experiment, but there are only 37 trading activities in a total of 832 trading days. Nevertheless, the trading activities are at least 229 with a greater than 5.8 percent average annual return when the predicted period is 20 and 30 days.

Compared to Table 4.6, Table 4.7 has fewer trading activities. Considering a 0.3-percent trading cost with $\tau = 1\%$, there are more than 130 trading activities with an annual return of greater than 10 percent in a 30-day-ahead forecasting period. Actually, empirical results in Table 4.5, Table 4.6, and Table 4.7 indicate that with the growth of critical number τ, the trading activities decrease.

As shown above in Table 4.6, in terms of MSE and D_{stat}, we select the best models to forecasting l-day-ahead predictions where $l = 1, 5, 10, 20,$ and 30. The third column shows the sample size in each model and is denoted as N_S. By the trading strategy rule in Equation 4.11 with $\tau = 0.5\%$, we generate N_S l-day returns. The

Table 4.7 Performance of trading strategy with $\tau = 1\%$ based on EMD-MLP.

				Return with transaction cost %			
		N_s	SD	0.0%	0.1%	0.2%	0.3%
Panel A: Best models (MSE)							
5-day	EMD(-1)-MLP(3)*	5	4.93	85.02	80.02	75.02	70.02
10-day	EMD(-1)-MLP(5,3)*	17	4.72	40.20	37.70	35.20	32.70
20-day	EMD(0)-MLP(5,3)*	78	2.19	18.38	17.13	15.88	14.63
30-day	EMD(-1)-MLP(5,3)*	133	1.72	12.95	12.12	11.29	10.45
Panel B: Best models (D_{stat})							
5-day	EMD(-1)-MLP(5,3)*	7	5.92	67.03	62.03	57.03	52.03
10-day	EMD(-1)-MLP(5,3)*	17	4.72	40.20	37.70	35.20	32.70
20-day	EMD(0)-MLP(3)*	69	2.32	18.43	17.18	15.93	14.68
30-day	EMD(-2)-MLP(5,3)*	131	1.72	13.08	12.24	11.41	10.58

fourth column reports the standard deviation of the annualized returns without transaction cost. The last four columns represent the averages of N_S annualized returns with different transaction costs.

As shown in Table 4.7, in terms of MSE and D_{stat}, we select the best models to forecasting l-day-ahead predictions where $l = 1$, 5, 10, 20, and 30. The third column shows the sample size in each model and is denoted as N_S. By the trading strategy rule in Equation 4.11 with $\tau = 1\%$, we generate N_S l-day returns. The fourth column reports the standard deviation of the annualized returns without transaction costs. The last four columns represent the averages of N_S annualized returns with different transaction costs.

4.4 Conclusion

This chapter investigates the forecasting models for the RMB exchange rate and proposes related trading strategies based on the constructed models, which is not only meaningful to Chinese investment institutions and policymakers, but also to anyone interested in the RMB currency or RMB-related products.

We consider both the CNY and CNH exchange rates and apply the model of EMD-MLP with different forecasting horizons to forecast RMB exchange rates. Apart from different critical numbers, different trading costs are also considered in the process of proposing suitable trading strategies. Then, we perform experiments that are used to examine the performance of the forecasting models and trading strategies. This chapter introduces three models including the MLP model, the hybrid EMD-MLP model, and the EMD-MLP*. Based on the MLP model, we propose the hybrid EMD-MLP and EMD-MLP* models which consider different levels of frequency of IMFs to improve forecasting performance. When we forecast RMB exchange rates based on both MSE and D_{stat} criteria, empirical results show that if the forecasting period is five days or longer, the hybrid EMD-MLP* model performs best among these selected models.

Next, we introduce both different critical numbers and trading costs to test the performance of trading strategies with l-day-ahead predictions. According to the test results, if the critical number is equal to zero, which means that the annual returns mainly become negative, the trading strategy will be abandoned; if τ does not equal zero, then as the forecasting periods increase, the annual return decreases.

Generally speaking, the hybrid EMD-MLP and EMD-MLP* models are more suitable for proposing trading strategies over longer forecasting horizons – for instance, 20 days ahead or 30 days ahead.

Compared to shorter forecasting horizons, though the annual return in longer forecasting horizons is limited, the amount of trading activities is proper. When $\tau = 1\%$, the annual return of trading strategy is more than 10 percent and trading opportunities are at least 130.

Notes

1   This report shows that the gross domestic product based on purchasing-power-parity valuation of country GDP of China is $18.088 billion compared to the United States ($17.348 billion). The source website is www.imf. org/data.
2   The stopping rule indicates that absolute values of envelope mean must be less than the user-specified tolerance level. In this study, the tolerance level is denoted as the standard deviation of $x(t)$ times 0.01.
3   Since the cases of CNY and CNH (from 2011 to 2015) produced similar results, we do not report them in this paper.

5 Hedging currency risk

5.1 Introduction

In terms of purchasing power parity, China has surpassed the United States to become the world's largest economy in 2014, reported by International Monetary Fund (IMF) in 2015.[1] Therefore, the RMB, as the official currency of China, has attracted global attention from policymakers, investment institutions, and entrepreneurs. Recent years have witnessed the increasing global influence of the RMB. According to the Society of Worldwide Interbank Financial Telecommunication (SWIFT), in August 2015 the RMB overtook the Japanese yen to become one of the top four world payment currencies. However, relative to the top three currencies, including the US dollar (44.89 percent), euro (27.2 percent), and British pound (8.5 percent), the RMB accounted for only 2.8 percent of total global payments in August 2015.

Based on the increasing influence of Chinese international trade and investment, internationalizing the RMB is an indispensable duty—not only for China, but also for the rest of the world. The internationalization of the RMB is not only beneficial for the stability of China's financial industry, but also for the diversification of the global reserve system and the balance of the global financial system. Since the impact of the 2008 financial crisis, more countries have been improving the diversification of international reserve currency. Thus, with the internationalization of the RMB, it is possible for the RMB to become reserve currency. At the same time, in order to promote international use of the RMB in trade, investment, and asset management, the government has taken many measures, including the liberation of capital accounts, RMB interest rates, and exchange rate system reform. Besides, more currency swap agreements with other countries' central banks are being reached; on 1 October 2016, the RMB was formally included in the IMF's Special Drawing Rights (SDR), where the RMB has a weighting of 10.92 percent in the new SDR basket.

According to Cui (2014), in order to achieve the goal of becoming an international currency, the RMB should go through three steps: settlement currency, denomination currency, and reserve currency. It is worth noting that the first RMB offshore center was established in Hong Kong. In December 2008, Chinese Premier Wen Jiabao announced the creation of a pilot program for cross-border trade settlement of the RMB with Hong Kong. The RMB officially became deliverable in Hong Kong on 19 July 2010, with a joint announcement between the People's Bank of China (PBOC) and the Hong Kong Monetary Authority (HKMA). Thus, the market for CNH (i.e. the offshore-traded RMB) had officially commenced. As shown in Figure 5.1, due to the rapid growth of the CNH, Hong Kong has become the largest RMB liquidity pool outside mainland China. Compared to the fourth quarter in 2010, RMB deposits in Hong Kong increased more than two times and reached more than US$ 2.9 trillion at the second quarter of 2015, as reported by HKMA.

Many studies have shown the relationship between CNY and CNH exchange rates, such as the study from Cheung and Rime (2014) based on a specialized microstructure dataset, which indicates that both the CNH exchange rate and the CNH flow have an increasing impact on the exchange rate of CNY, and the interactions between CNY and CNH are time-varying. Funke et al. (2015) expounded on the role of liquidity in driving the differential between CNY and CNH exchange rates by applying extended GARCH models. However, studies from

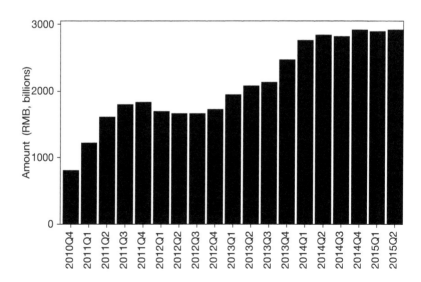

Figure 5.1 The RMB deposits in Hong Kong from 2010 Q4 to 2015 Q2.

Lustig et al. (2011), Lustig and Verdelhan (2007), and Verdelhan (2012) all propose the existence of systematic risk in exchange rates. Thus, currency hedging is indispensable and now many studies have been involved in the research field. Compared with the risk–return performances of diversified portfolios with and without forward contract hedging, Glen and Jorion (1993) found that the portfolios including forward contracts perform significantly better than the unhedged portfolios. Based on the framework of Glen and Jorion (1993), who consider the issue of minimizing the risk of global equity and bond market investors between 1975 and 2005, Campbell et al. (2010) concluded that the standard deviation of unhedged portfolios is reduced by introducing the optimal currency hedging strategy. Allayannis and Ofek (2001) studied whether companies choose foreign exchange derivatives to hedge or speculate and find that hedging using derivatives significantly reduces the company's exchange rate risk.

Kroencke and Schindler (2012) extended the range of investments from international equity and bond markets to securitized real estate and broadly considered the effects of currency risk. By adding international real estate to stocks and bond portfolios, the authors show that the shift of the mean variance boundary is conditional on currency hedged and unhedged portfolios.[2] By investigating the performance of cross-hedging, Wei and Dark (2015) explained that natural hedges, by using a dynamic approach, could improve hedging performance. The theoretical and empirical evidence of a model, proposed by Gatopoulos and Loubergé (2013), show that financial derivatives are effective for a firm's hedging in Latin America. When it came to hedging in stressful times in G10 countries, Hossfeld and Macdonald (2015) found safe-haven currencies by using a threshold regression approach. Hau (2014) examined the structure of exchange arbitrage strategies and proposed the importance of foreign exchange hedging. Considering the increasing importance of the Chinese economy and its official currency, the RMB, it is possible that the RMB could become the international currency in the near future. By applying the model of a three-country, three-currency portfolio, Bénassy-Quéré and Forouheshfar (2015) examined the impact of RMB internationalization on exchange rates.

What this paper will explain is the following: first, with economic globalization, the wealth growth of Chinese individuals, and the internationalization of the RMB, more Chinese institutions and individuals tend to possess foreign assets including foreign currencies, foreign bonds, and other foreign real estate. Also, most import and export enterprises are inclined to choose the USD as the settlement currency of the international transaction. In fact, all individuals and businesses participating in international activities have to bear the foreign exchange rate risk. Second, as the RMB continues to internationalize, the risk of foreign exchange rates is higher. Since the reform of the RMB exchange rate regime in 2005, the Chinese government continually allows the RMB to fluctuate in a wider range. From the latest announcement published on 17 March 2014, RMB allowance to float in the band was extended to 2 percent. Besides, with the increasing use of the RMB in international activities, the liquidity of RMB currency has increased as well. There is no doubt that a wider range of volatility and more liquidity of the RMB are accompanied by more exchange rate risk. Thus, the third question we need to discuss is how to hedge the currency risk with the approach of derivatives and forward contracts for Chinese investors.[3]

The above problems will be explored in this paper by comparing the performance of hedged and unhedged foreign investment portfolios, where both portfolios are constructed from ten different datasets. In order to avoid incomplete and unreliable results, both equal-weighted portfolios and optimal-weighted portfolios are used to examine the portfolio performance. We also introduce the Sharpe ratio, which considers both return and risk, to measure the portfolios' performances. Furthermore, we follow preceding studies – including Fleming et al. (2001, 2003) and Bandi and Russell (2006) – to calculate the economic benefits of fully hedged portfolios compared to unhedged ones; that is, how much a risk-averse investor would be willing to pay using a fully hedged portfolio. Finally, the efficient frontiers and time-varying rolling estimations will be used to explore more evidence about the hedging effects.

The rest of this paper is organized in the following manner. Section 5.2 introduces the methodology related to currency hedging, assets allocation and how to measure the Sharpe ratio and economic benefit. Section 5.3 describes the empirical studies in detail, where we compare the performance of fully hedged and unhedged portfolios consisting of ten datasets. Section 5.4 concludes this chapter.

5.2 Methodology

5.2.1 Currency hedging

As mentioned in Section 5.1, more Chinese individuals and institutions are inclined to possess foreign assets based on the US dollar, and other countries' investors also hold assets in the RMB. So, how to hedge currency risk becomes an important issue. Therefore, this study focuses on the perspective of the Chinese investor, who deals with foreign assets in

US dollars, and we will explore how to hedge the currency risk by using forward exchange rate market data. The currency-unhedged returns are measured as:

$$r_{U,t+1} = \frac{P_{t+1}S_{t+1}}{P_t S_t} - 1 \tag{5.1}$$

where P_t is the price of the foreign asset in US dollars and S_t is the RMB spot price of one US dollar. In empirical studies, S_t could be found from the CNY and CNH spot rates. In order to decompose the currency-unhedged return, $r_{t+1} = P_{t+1} / P_t - 1$ is defined as the asset returns in US dollars, and $s_{t+1} = S_{t+1} / S_t - 1$ is defined as the exchange rate component. Then, Equation 5.1 could be rewritten as:

$$r_{U,t+1} = (P_{t+1} / P_t - 1) + (S_{t+1} / S_t - 1) + (P_{t+1} / P_t - 1)(S_{t+1} / S_t - 1)$$
$$= r_{t+1} + s_{t+1} + r_{t+1}s_{t+1}, \tag{5.2}$$

where $r_{t+1}s_{t+1}$ is a cross-product component.

According to Kroencke and Schindler (2012), several financial derivatives, such as forward contracts, swap contracts, and futures, could be used for hedging currency risk. And we choose forward contracts, which are more popular and easy to obtain, to study risk hedging in this chapter. Let $F_{t|t+1}$ be the one-period forward contract price of the exchange rate; then the return of a currency long-forward contract could be calculated by $(S_{t+1} - F_{t|t+1}) / S_t$. Using a simple hedging strategy produces the currency-hedged returns expressed as:

$$r_{H,t+1} = r_{U,t+1} - \psi(\frac{S_{t+1} - F_{t|t+1}}{S_t}) \tag{5.3}$$

where ψ is the hedging ratio parameter. Generally, a smaller ψ produces fewer currency risks. In this study, we use a fully hedged strategy that defines ψ in Equation 5.3 to explain currency risk. At present, several studies including Eun and Resnick (1988), Peroldandre and Schulmanevan (1988), and Jorion (1994) have proposed the optimal hedging strategy, but the fully hedged strategy may still be seen as a fair benchmark to measure hedging performance. Given the forward premium $\psi = 1$, the fully hedged return $(f_{t|t+1} = F_{t|t+1} / S_t - 1)$ can be written as:

$$
\begin{aligned}
r_{H,t+1} &= r_{t+1} + s_{t+1} + r_{t+1}s_{t+1} - 1 \times \left((s_{t+1} + 1) - (f_{t|t+1} + 1) \right) \\
&= r_{t+1} + f_{t|t+1} + r_{t+1}s_{t+1}.
\end{aligned}
\tag{5.4}
$$

So, compared to Equation 5.2, Equation 5.4 takes the forward premium $f_{t|t+1}$ and the uncertain exchange rate component s_{t+1} into account.

5.2.2 Assets allocation

It is well known that applying appropriate assets allocation usually could diversify the individual risks. Based on returns and variances of portfolio, Markowitz (1952) proposed the optimal rule in modern portfolio theory, which is used to decide each risky asset's weight. Many studies have proposed different or improved assets allocation approaches, such as the Bayesian diffuse-prior portfolio in Barry (1974), Klein and Bawa (1976), and Brown (1979), the Bayesian portfolio based on belief models in Pastor and Stambaugh (2000), unobservable factors and asset-pricing models in MacKinlay and Pástor (2000), and the mean-VaR model in Alexander and Baptista (2002). Also, based on 14 models and seven empirical datasets, DeMiguel et al. (2009) examined out-of-sample portfolio performance, and found that the equal-weighted portfolio model is suitable to evaluate the Sharpe ratio, certainty-equivalent return, or turnover. Thus, the equal-weighted rule is also used in our study to construct the fully hedged and unhedged portfolios. According to the equal-weighted rule, a portfolio consisting of N risky assets could be equally divided into N copies, that is, each asset's weight is fixed in $1/N$.

Formally, given a dataset consisting of N risky assets with T periods, by Equations 5.4 and 5.2, the fully hedged and unhedged returns of asset i at t period are defined as $r_{H,t}^i$ and $r_{U,t}^i$, where $t = 1, 2, \ldots, T$ and $i = 1, 2, \ldots, N$. According the equal-weighted strategy, the fully hedged and unhedged portfolio returns are calculated by:

$$
R_{H,t} = \frac{1}{N} \sum_{i=1}^{N} r_{H,t}^i, t = 1, 2, \ldots, T
\tag{5.5}
$$

$$R_{U,t} = \frac{1}{N} \sum_{i=1}^{N} r^i{}_{U,t}, t = 1, 2, \ldots, T \tag{5.6}$$

In addition to the equal-weighted portfolios, the rolling-sample approach is also further applied to build the optimal-weighted portfolios for evaluating hedging performance. To be specific, given a dataset of asset returns with T periods, an estimation window of length M is discussed. In each period, where t starts from $T = M + 1$, in order to achieve the maximum Sharpe ratio or expected utility, we will use the previous M periods to evaluate the optimal weights of each asset, i.e., w_k^{1*}, w_k^{2*}, ..., w_k^{N*}, $k = H$ or U. Then we use these optimal weights to find the portfolio return at $t = M + 1$. This process is continued from $t = M + 1$ to T. Thus, an optimal-weighted portfolio returns series is obtained by the method of rolling-sample. Formally, the fully hedged and unhedged portfolio returns are computed by:

$$R^*{}_{H,t} = \sum_{i=1}^{N} w^{i*}{}_{H,t} r^i_{H,t}, \ t = M + 1, M + 2, \ldots, T, \tag{5.7}$$

$$R^*{}_{U,t} = \sum_{i=1}^{N} w^{i*}_{U,t} r^i{}_{U,t}, \ t = M + 1, M + 2, \ldots, T, \tag{5.8}$$

where $w^{i*}{}_{H,t}$ and $w^{i*}_{U,t}$ are the optimal asset weights estimated by the previous M periods for fully hedged and unhedged returns.

5.2.3 Sharpe ratio

The Sharpe ratio not only takes return and risk simultaneously into account when measuring portfolio performance, but also proposes that a portfolio's excess returns are decided by asset allocation or just holding too much risk. A higher Sharpe ratio indicates the portfolio has better risk-adjusted performance. In this paper, we adopt the Sharpe ratio to evaluate the performance of fully hedged and unhedged portfolios. This chapter introduces the Sharpe ratio to estimate fully-hedged and unhedged portfolio performances. Specifically, consider the equal-weighted strategy; the Sharpe ratios of fully hedged and unhedged portfolios are calculated by:

$$SR_k = \frac{\hat{\mu}_k}{\hat{\sigma}_k}, k = H \text{ and U} \qquad (5.9)$$

where $\hat{\mu}_k$ is the mean of excess returns and $\hat{\sigma}_k$ is the standard deviation. Due to the weekly risk-free returns being very close to zero, there was no need to adjust the excess returns in our empirical studies. In the meantime, our study tests the null hypothesis to examine whether the Sharpe ratios of fully hedged and unhedged portfolios are statistically distinguishable. And the alternative hypotheses are expressed as:

$$H_0 : SR_H - SR_U = 0,$$
$$H_a : SR_H - SR_U \neq 0.$$

By Equation 5.9, the above hypotheses can be rewritten as

$$H_0 : \hat{\mu}_H \hat{\sigma}_U - \hat{\mu}_U \hat{\sigma}_H = 0,$$
$$H_a : \hat{\mu}_H \hat{\sigma}_U - \hat{\mu}_U \hat{\sigma}_H \neq 0.$$

According to Jobson and Korkie (1981) and Memmel (2003), we calculate the test statistic $\hat{z}_{JK}$, which is an asymptotically standard normal distribution:

$$\hat{z}_{JK} = \frac{\hat{\mu}_H \hat{\sigma}_U - \hat{\mu}_U \hat{\sigma}_H}{\sqrt{\hat{\vartheta}}} \qquad (5.10)$$

With

$$\hat{\vartheta} = \frac{1}{T} \left(2\hat{\sigma}_U^2 \hat{\sigma}_H^2 - 2\hat{\sigma}_H \hat{\sigma}_U \hat{\sigma}_{H,U} + \frac{1}{2} \hat{\mu}_H^2 \hat{\sigma}_U^2 + \frac{1}{2} \hat{\mu}_U^2 \hat{\sigma}_H^2 - \frac{\hat{\mu}_H \hat{\mu}_U}{\hat{\sigma}_H \hat{\sigma}_U} \hat{\sigma}_{H,U}^2 \right) \qquad (5.11)$$

It is worth noting that $1/(T - M)$ is to substitute for $1/T$ when we estimate $\hat{\vartheta}$ in the optimal-weighted cases. Based on the test statistic $\hat{z}_{JK}$, the p-value of the difference between SR_H and SR_U in our empirical studies will be reported in Section 5.3.

5.2.4 Economic benefit

For the sake of evaluating the value of hedging, we compare the performance of the fully hedged portfolio to the unhedged portfolio. Fleming et al. (2001, 2003) and Bandi and Russell (2006) propose the idea of economic benefit measuring, which is also used and further extended in our study. When hedging cannot generate economic benefit, the utility of the fully hedged or unhedged portfolios are statistically equal. Referring to Fleming et al. (2001), we can use the quadratic utility, which can be seen as a second-order approximation to the investor's utility function, to weigh the economic benefit:

$$U\left(W_{t+1}\right) = W_t R_{t+1} - \frac{\alpha W_t^2}{2} R_{t+1}^2 \tag{5.12}$$

where W_t is the investor's wealth at t, α is his absolute risk aversion, and R_{t+1} is his portfolio return at $t + 1$. In order to simplify Equation 5.12, αW_t is defined as a fixed constant and then γ, the investor's relative risk aversion, is equal to $\alpha W_t / (1 - \alpha W_t)$. So, we use the average realized utility $\bar{U}(\cdot)$ of the fully hedged and unhedged portfolio to measure the expected utility. To be specific, given an investor who uses the equal-weighted strategy, his expected utilities of fully hedged and unhedged portfolios are calculated by:

$$\bar{U}(R_H) = W_0 \times \sum_{t=1}^{T} \left(R_{H,t} - \frac{\gamma}{2(1+\gamma)} R_{H,t}^2 \right) \tag{5.13}$$

$$\bar{U}(R_U) = W_0 \times \sum_{t=1}^{T} \left(R_{U,t} - \frac{\gamma}{2(1+\gamma)} R_{U,t}^2 \right) \tag{5.14}$$

where W_0 is the investor's initial wealth. Similarly, the evaluated economic benefit of currency hedging is equal to the average utilities of fully hedged and unhedged portfolios. Therefore, we need to compute the cost of the fully hedged portfolio to determine for an investor whether or not it is necessary to hedge currency risk. The parameter of Δ is defined as the maximum fee that investors would be willing to pay for hedging, and then we can decide the value of Δ that satisfies:

$$\sum_{t=1}^{T}\left((R_{H,t} - \Delta) - \frac{\gamma}{2(1+\gamma)}(R_{H,t} - \Delta)^2\right) = \sum_{t=1}^{T}(R_{U,t} - \frac{\gamma}{2(1+\gamma)}R_{U,t}^2) \quad (5.15)$$

It can be rewritten as:

$$\frac{\gamma}{2(1+\gamma)}\Delta^2 + \left(1 - \frac{\gamma}{(1+\gamma)}\hat{\mu}_H\right)\Delta - \Psi = 0 \quad (5.16)$$

where $\hat{\mu}_H$ is the mean of the fully hedged portfolio's returns. Ψ, the difference of average utilities, is defined as:

$$\Psi = \frac{1}{T}\sum_{t=1}^{T}(R_{H,t} - \frac{\gamma}{2(1+\gamma)}R_{H,t}^2) - \frac{1}{T}\sum_{t=1}^{T}(R_{U,t} - \frac{\gamma}{2(1+\gamma)}R_{U,t}^2) \quad (5.17)$$

Finally, the value of Δ can be calculated by:

$$\Delta = \frac{1+\gamma}{\gamma}\left[\left(\frac{\gamma}{1+\gamma}\hat{\mu}_H - 1\right) + \sqrt{\left(1 - \frac{\gamma}{1+\gamma}\hat{\mu}_H\right)^2 + \frac{2\gamma}{1+\gamma}\Psi}\right] \quad (5.18)$$

The other solution, which does not always make sense economically, is ignored in our study. The values of Δ, which are measured by using three different values of γ – that is, 1, 5, and 10 – are reported as annualized economic benefit in basis points.

5.3 Empirical studies

5.3.1 *Data and statistics descriptions*

In this empirical section, we try to verify the importance of RMB hedging. Based on the same ten datasets, we design the fully hedged and unhedged portfolios to estimate hedging performance. The ten datasets are listed in Table 5.1. The table lists ten datasets in which each dataset includes weekly data of N risky assets ranging from 2 January 2006 to 31 December 2014. The first six datasets include size and book-to-market dataset [DS(S-B)], size and investment dataset [DS(S-I)], size and operating profitability dataset [DS(S-O)], industry dataset [DS(Ind)], momentum dataset [DS(Mom)], and long-term reversal dataset [DS(Rev)]. These are downloaded from Ken French's website (http://mba.tuck.dartmouth.edu/pages/faculty/ken.french/). For example, considering the industry dataset [DS(Ind)] with ten portfolios, we assign NYSE, AMEX, and NASDAQ stocks to an industry portfolio. These ten industry portfolios with shocks are seen as risky assets that are then used to construct the fully hedged or unhedged portfolio. We can find more formal and detailed definitions of them.

Table 5.1 Dataset description and source.

#	Dataset Description	N	Source	Abbreviation
1	Portfolios Formed on Size and Book-to-Market	6	Ken French's Website	DS(S-B)
2	Portfolios Formed on Size and Investment	6	Ken French's Website	DS(S-I)
3	Portfolios Formed on Size and Operating Profitability	6	Ken French's Website	DS(S-O)
4	Industry Portfolios	10	Ken French's Website	DS(Ind)
5	Portfolios Formed on Momentum	10	Ken French's Website	DS(Mom)
6	Portfolios Formed on Long-Term Reversal	10	Ken French's Website	DS(Rev)
7	VTI+VBR+VUG+VGK+XLV+EFA+EWJ	7	Yahoo! Finance	DS(ETF1)
8	AGG+VO+VBK+VWO+XLK+TIP+GLD	7	Yahoo! Finance	DS(ETF2)

(*continued*)

Table 5.1 Dataset description and source (*continued*).

#	Dataset Description	N	Source	Abbreviation
9	VB+VTV+VNQ+LQD+XLF+XLE+DVY	7	Yahoo! Finance	DS(ETF3)
10	D(ETF1)+D(ETF2)+D(ETF3)	21	Yahoo! Finance	DS(ETF0)

Table 5.1 lists the ten datasets used in the empirical studies. Each dataset contains N risky assets in which sample periods are from 2 January 2006 to 31 December 2014. Datasets #1–6 were produced from Ken French's website. Datasets #7–10 consist of 21 popular Exchange Traded Funds (ETFs), which are included in 21 different categories and can be downloaded from Yahoo! Finance (http://finance.yahoo.com/etfs). The detailed descriptions about the ETF assets are reported in Table 5.2. In the last column is the abbreviation used to refer to the datasets in all content evaluating the hedging performance. In the last two columns are the means and standard deviations of weekly returns for each ETF.

As we know, an ETF is a marketable security tracking an index, a commodity, bonds, or a basket of assets. Investors can short-sell ETF shares or hold for the long term, as long as they pay a certain percentage of the margin.

The selection of ETFs proceeds as follows: first, we choose the top 50 ETFs that are traded in the US with the largest size (net assets) on 10 August 2015. Second, we deduct the ETFs with an inception date after 1 January 2006, which do not match our sample period. Finally, for each category, only the ETF with the lowest expense ratio remains. More detailed introductions about these ETFs are provided in Table 5.2. The table lists the 21 most popular ETFs used in the datasets D(ETF1), D(ETF2), D(ETF3), and D(ETF4). The sample period is from 2 January 2006 to 31 December 2014.

This chapter mainly discusses the hedging of RMB exchange rate risks, so we introduce the RMB foreign exchange rate data. As mentioned in Chapter 1, the RMB includes the CNY and CNH, in which the CNY is traded onshore (mainland China) and the CNY is traded offshore (mainly in Hong Kong). Therefore, two kinds of currency exchange rates, USD to CNY and USD to CNH, are introduced in this empirical study. Also, the CNYF and CNHF, which are the corresponding one-week RMB non-deliverable forwards (NDF) in the onshore and offshore markets, are available. Furthermore, we define the midquote between the end-of-day quoted ask and the bid rates as the price of the empirical exchange rate or forward. More descriptions about currency rates are provided in Figures 5.2 and 5.3, in which all data are downloaded from Bloomberg.

Table 5.2 List of the exchange traded funds considered.

#	ETF NAME	TICKER	CATEGORY	NET ASSETS	INCEPTION	Mean %	Stdev %
1	Vanguard Total Stock Market ETF	VTI	Large Blend	410.77B	2001-05-24	0.184	2.720
2	Vanguard Small-Cap Value ETF	VBR	Small Value	16.98B	2004-01-26	0.210	3.343
3	Vanguard Growth ETF	VUG	Large Growth	48.71B	2004-01-26	0.193	2.594
4	Vanguard FTSE Europe ETF	VGK	Europe Stock	20.9B	2005-03-04	0.124	3.376
5	Health Care Select Sector SPDR ETF	XLV	Health	14.51B	1998-12-16	0.219	2.238
6	iShares MSCI EAFE	EFA	Foreign Large Blend	61.59B	2001-08-14	0.098	3.069
7	iShares MSCI Japan	EWJ	Japan Stock	19.24B	1996-03-12	0.016	2.769
8	iShares Core US Aggregate Bond	AGG	Intermediate-Term Bond	24.89B	2003-09-22	0.092	0.768

(*continued*)

Table 5.2 List of the exchange traded funds considered (*continued*).

#	ETF NAME	TICKER	CATEGORY	NET ASSETS	INCEPTION	Mean %	Stdev %
9	Vanguard Mid-Cap ETF	VO	Mid-Cap Blend	66.29B	2004-01-26	0.206	3.088
10	Vanguard Small-Cap Growth ETF	VBK	Small Growth	17.01B	2004-01-26	0.226	3.368
11	Vanguard FTSE Emerging Markets ETF	VWO	Diversified Emerging Mkts	66.78B	2005-03-04	0.163	3.765
12	Technology Select Sector SPDR ETF	XLK	Technology	13.54B	1998-12-16	0.199	2.709
13	iShares TIPS Bond	TIP	Inflation-Protected Bond	13.9B	2003-12-04	0.087	0.930
14	SPDR Gold Shares	GLD	Commodities Precious Metals	27.41B	2004-11-18	0.198	2.751
15	Vanguard Small-Cap ETF	VB	Small Blend	56.16B	2004-01-26	0.219	3.313
16	Vanguard Value ETF	VTV	Large Value	38.64B	2004-01-26	0.168	2.746
17	Vanguard REIT ETF	VNQ	Real Estate	50.17B	2004-09-23	0.229	4.195
18	iShares iBoxx $ Invst Grade Crp Bond	LQD	Corporate Bond	22.13B	2002-07-22	0.116	1.046
19	Financial Select Sector SPDR ETF	XLF	Financial	18.1B	1998-12-16	0.088	4.613

(*continued*)

Table 5.2 List of the exchange traded funds considered (*continued*).

#	ETF NAME	TICKER	CATEGORY	NET ASSETS	INCEPTION	Mean %	Stdev %
20	Energy Select Sector SPDR ETF	XLE	Equity Energy	13.36B	1998-12-16	0.189	3.795
21	iShares Select Dividend	DVY	Mid-Cap Value	14.76B	2003-11-03	0.160	2.791

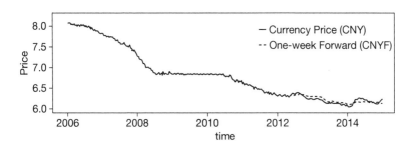

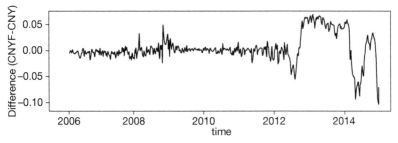

Figure 5.2 Time trends in CNY and CNYF.

The time trends of the CNY and CNYF with periods from 2 January 2006 to 31 December 2014 are displayed in Figure 5.2. Since the offshore market was established formally in 2010, the trends in the CNH and CNHF, with shorter periods ranging from 9 September 2010 to 31 December 2014, are provided in Figure 5.3. Both figures also present the differences between current exchange rates and the corresponding NDF, which shows that the differences in the onshore market are much larger than in the offshore market.

Figure 5.2 plots time trends of both the currency price (CNY) and its one-week forward contract price (CNYF). The following figure shows the difference between the CNYF and the CNY. The sample covers weekly data, and the period ranges from 2 January 2006 to 31 December 2014.

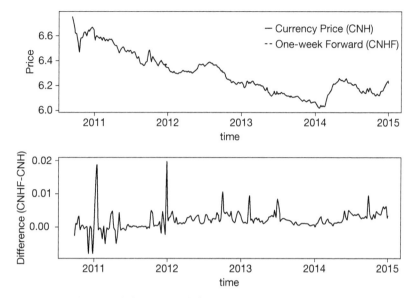

Figure 5.3 Time trends in CNH and CNHF.

Figure 5.3 plots time trends of both the currency price (CNH) and its one-week forward contract price (CNHF). The following figure shows the difference between CNHF and CNH. The sample covers weekly data, and the period ranges from 9 September 2010 to 31 December 2014.

We compute the weekly CNY, CNYF, CNH, and CNHF returns by subtracting one from price relatives. Table 5.3 presents the returns. From Table 5.3, we can find that the sample full period is divided into Period 1 and Period 2, shown in Panel B and Panel C, respectively. The reason is that CNHF data is available starting from 8 September 2010. The mean, standard deviation (Stdev), maximum (Max), minimum (Min), skewness, and kurtosis of weekly returns are all provided in Table 5.3. The experimental results of means show that both the CNY and CNH exchange rate to USD appreciated during the empirical period. However, compared to the speed of appreciation in Period 1 shown in Panel B of Table 5.3, the speed of appreciation slows down in Period 2. In the meantime, we find that the volatility of the RMB exchange rate in Period 2 is larger than in Period 1 and the CNH has larger volatility than the CNY from the values of Stdev.

Table 5.3 provides summary statistics for weekly returns on CNY, CNYF, CNH, and CNHF. The returns are computed as weekly price

Table 5.3 Summary statistics for weekly CNY, CNYF, CNH, and CNHF returns.

	Observations	Mean %	Stdev%	Max%	Min%	Skewness	Kurtosis	Correlation
Panel A: Full-period (2006-01-03 to 2014-12-31)								
CNY	468	0.056	0.212	1.234	−0.973	0.164	5.172	0.700
CNYF	468	−0.058	0.200	0.665	−1.133	−0.687	3.071	–
Panel B: Period 1 (2006-01-03 to 2010-09-07)								
CNY	244	−0.070	0.182	0.680	−0.865	−0.838	3.055	0.821
CNYF	244	−0.070	0.188	0.513	−0.746	−0.564	1.750	–
Panel C: Period 2 (2010-09-08 to 2014-12-31)								
CNY	224	−0.036	0.232	1.234	−0.790	0.849	4.926	0.577
CNYF	224	−0.040	0.201	0.665	−0.800	−0.342	1.969	–
CNH	224	−0.033	0.335	2.125	−1.171	1.011	8.801	0.978
CNHF	224	−0.033	0.326	2.117	−1.171	1.306	9.391	–

relatives minus one. CNY and CNH refer to trade onshore (in mainland China) and offshore (mainly through Hong Kong), respectively. In the onshore and offshore markets, we denote the one-week RMB non-deliverable forwards (NDF) as CNYF and CNHF, respectively. Because CNHF is available from 8 September 2010 in Bloomberg, we divide the full period (3 January 2006 to 31 December 2014) into two sub-periods based on this date. We report the mean, standard deviation (Stdev), maximum (Max), minimum (Min), skewness, and kurtosis of weekly returns. The last column is the correlation coefficients of currency returns and the corresponding forward returns.

5.3.2 Equal-weighted portfolios

First, we apply the equal-weighted strategies to measure the hedging effects. Based on the equal-weighted strategy among ten datasets, we use Equation 5.9, introduced in Section 5.2, to evaluate the Sharpe ratios of fully hedged and unhedged portfolios. Table 5.4 shows the Sharpe ratios, in which the differences between the fully hedged and unhedged portfolios' Sharpe ratios are also provided. The p-values showed in the last line of each panel in Table 5.4 are calculated by Equation 5.10 based on the null hypothesis $H_0 : SR_H - SR_U = 0$. The empirical results of CNY in Period 1 show that the difference between fully hedged and unhedged portfolios – that is, the hedge effects – is significantly positive in all datasets (p-value < 0.05) and the average is 0.0081. Focusing on Panels B and C of Table 5.4, we see that the average differences of the CNY and the CNH are 0.0607 and 0.0268 respectively, which indicates the hedge effects of both the CNY and the CNH become more significantly positive (p < 0.01).

The economic benefits of fully hedged and unhedged portfolios based on the equal-weighted strategy are considered in Table 5.4. The values of Δ estimated by Equation 5.16 – that is, the basis points with three different values of γ, 1, 5, and 10 multiplied by 52 – are regarded as the annualized economic benefit. Whether in Period 1 or 2, the empirical results of $\gamma = 1, 5, 10$ are similar and only the case of $\gamma = 5$ is discussed in this section. For Period 1 in Panel A, the average economic benefit of CNY is 137.6 bps while it rises sharply to 759.6 bps in Period 2. Panel C shows the average economic benefit of the CNH is 336.5 bps when $\gamma = 5$. The average economic benefits of 759.6 bps and 336.5 bps indicate that, compared to Period 1, investors are willing to pay more than 5.5 times and 2.4 times the fees for constructing the

Table 5.4 Sharpe ratios for equal-weighted portfolios.

Dataset	S-B	S-I	S-O	Ind	Mom	Rev	ETF1	ETF2	ETF3	ETF0	Average
Panel A: Period 1 (CNY)											
fully-hedged	0.0260	0.0244	0.0242	0.0363	0.0385	0.0204	−0.0061	0.0499	0.0034	0.0121	0.0229
Unhedged	0.0187	0.0168	0.0167	0.0277	0.0316	0.0123	−0.0141	0.0387	−0.0038	0.0033	0.0148
Difference	0.0073	0.0076	0.0075	0.0086	0.0069	0.0082	0.0080	0.0112	0.0072	0.0087	0.0081
p-value	(0.0186)	(0.0186)	(0.0186)	(0.0191)	(0.0194)	(0.0184)	(0.0184)	(0.0189)	(0.0179)	(0.0179)	–
Panel B: Period 2 (CNY)											
fully-hedged	0.1790	0.1824	0.1780	0.2011	0.1804	0.1800	0.1786	0.1954	0.2053	0.1970	0.1877
Unhedged	0.1318	0.1349	0.1312	0.1482	0.1314	0.1313	0.1130	0.0983	0.1313	0.1188	0.1270
Difference	0.0472	0.0476	0.0468	0.0529	0.0491	0.0488	0.0656	0.0971	0.0740	0.0782	0.0607
p-value	(0.0021)	(0.0022)	(0.0021)	(0.0026)	(0.0021)	(0.0021)	(0.0006)	(0.0006)	(0.0006)	(0.0007)	–
Panel C: Period 2 (CNH)											
fully-hedged	0.1556	0.1590	0.1549	0.1754	0.1561	0.1559	0.1445	0.1460	0.1671	0.1569	0.1571
Unhedged	0.1338	0.1370	0.1333	0.1510	0.1337	0.1335	0.1167	0.1045	0.1358	0.1238	0.1303
Difference	0.0218	0.0220	0.0216	0.0244	0.0224	0.0224	0.0278	0.0415	0.0313	0.0331	0.0268
p-value	(0.0075)	(0.0076)	(0.0074)	(0.0089)	(0.0078)	(0.0076)	(0.0049)	(0.0054)	(0.0050)	(0.0055)	–

CNY and CNH fully hedged portfolios, respectively, in Period 2. From the perspective of the Sharpe ratio or economic benefit, we can draw the conclusion that it is necessary for investors who hold foreign risky assets in their portfolios to hedge currency risks during the internationalization of the RMB.

Table 5.5 reports the economic benefits of fully hedged and unhedged portfolios based on the equal-weighted strategy. We report the estimates of Δ by Equation 5.16 as the annualized economic benefit in basis points using three different values of γ: 1, 5, and 10. In Panel A, the sample period is from 2 January 2006 to 7 September 2010; we use CNY and its forward CNYF to account for the currency risks and compute the fully hedged and unhedged portfolio returns. Similarly, in Panels B and C, the sample period is from 8 September 2010 to 31 December 2014; CNY (CNYF) and CNH (CNHF) are considered. In the last column are the average economic benefits among ten datasets.

5.3.3 Optimal-weighted portfolios

Based on the optimal-weighted strategy, the Sharpe ratios of fully hedged and unhedged portfolios estimated by Equation 5.9 are provided in Table 5.6, in which the estimation window of length M is 100, the maximum allocation of each asset is 1, and the optimal weights are estimated by achieving the maximum Sharpe ratio.[4] The portfolio return in the next period is calculated by these optimal weights and this process is continued from $t = M + 1$ to T. Also, we provide the hedging effects, which are also known as the differences between fully hedged and unhedged portfolios' Sharpe ratios in Table 5.6. Based on the null hypothesis $H_0 : SR_H - SR_U = 0$, the p-values are shown in the last line of each panel in Table 5.6 are calculated by Equation 5.10. The empirical results presented in Panel A of Table 5.6 show that the average Sharpe ratios of fully hedged and unhedged portfolios are negative in Period 1, which means that the hedge effects based on the optimal-weighted strategy are negative. This is opposite to the equal-weighted strategy. Although fully hedged portfolios still have better Sharpe ratios than unhedged ones in eight datasets, only two datasets present a weakly significant difference and two datasets even have a negative difference. However, in Period 2, the average Sharpe ratios (CNY) of fully hedged and unhedged portfolios are 0.3054 and 0.1153, respectively. And the difference in each dataset is strongly significantly positive ($p < 0.01$). Focusing on the empirical results in Panel B and C, either for CNY or CNH, the average Sharpe ratios (CNY) of fully hedged and unhedged portfolios are positive and their differences of each dataset

Table 5.5 Economic benefit for equal-weighted portfolios.

Dataset	S-B	S-I	S-O	Ind	Mom	Rev	ETF1	ETF2	ETF3	ETF0	Average
Panel A: Period 1 (CNY)											
$\gamma = 1$	143.7	143.7	143.7	143.9	143.4	143.7	129.3	128.7	130.3	129.5	138.0
$\gamma = 5$	142.9	142.9	142.9	143.2	142.5	142.9	129.6	128.6	131.2	129.8	137.6
$\gamma = 10$	142.7	142.7	142.7	143.0	142.2	142.7	129.7	128.5	131.4	129.9	137.6
Panel B: Period 2 (CNY)											
$\gamma = 1$	733.6	733.6	733.4	734.5	734.1	733.9	808.8	810.9	810.7	810.1	764.4
$\gamma = 5$	727.9	728.0	727.6	729.5	728.7	728.5	804.3	807.8	807.4	806.5	759.6
$\gamma = 10$	726.6	726.7	726.3	728.3	727.5	727.3	803.3	807.1	806.7	805.7	758.6
Panel C: Period 2 (CNH)											
$\gamma = 1$	338.7	338.8	338.6	339.3	338.6	338.7	338.5	339.4	339.5	339.1	338.9
$\gamma = 5$	335.5	335.6	335.4	336.5	335.4	335.6	336.1	337.4	337.7	337.1	336.2
$\gamma = 10$	334.7	334.9	334.6	335.8	334.6	334.9	335.5	337.0	337.3	336.6	335.6

are also positive ($p < 0.01$). Averaging the values of difference in the CNY and CNH of Period 2, the average differences in CNY and CNH are 0.0659 bps and 0.1901 bps, respectively. Clearly, the Sharpe ratios' differences in CNH are much smaller than CNY cases, but all p-values in CNH are smaller than 0.01, which means fully hedged portfolios are still effective in Period 2.

Table 5.6 illustrates the Sharpe ratios, estimated by Equation 5.9, of fully hedged and unhedged portfolios based on the optimal-weighted strategy. Given the estimation window of length $M = 100$ and maximum allocation of each asset is 1, the optimal weights are estimated by achieving the maximum Sharpe ratio. We use these optimal weights to find the portfolio return at next period and this process is continued from $t = M + 1$ to T. Therefore, the optimal-weighted portfolio returns are available. The differences between fully hedged and unhedged portfolios' Sharpe ratios are also reported. In parentheses are the p-values based on the null hypothesis $H_0 : SR_H - SR_U = 0$, which is estimated by Equation 5.10. In Panel A, the sample period is from 2 January 2006 to 7 September 2010, we use the CNY and its forward CNYF to account for the currency risks and compute the fully hedged and unhedged portfolio returns. Similarly for Panel B or C, the sample period is from 8 September 2010 to 31 December 2014; CNY (CNYF) and CNH (CNHF) are considered. In the last column are the averages among ten datasets.

Table 5.7 presents the economic benefit of the optimal-weighted portfolios, in which the estimation window of length M is 100, the maximum allocation of each asset is 1, and the optimal weights are estimated by achieving the maximum expected utility defined as Equation 5.13 or 5.14. Similarly, we find the portfolio return at the next period by introducing these optimal weights, and this process is continued from $t = M + 1$ to T. The values of Δ estimated by Equation 5.16 – that is, the basis points with three different values of γ, 1, 5, and 10 multiplied by 52 – are regarded as annualized economic benefits. Since different γ produces similar results, this chapter only discusses the case of $= 5$. According to the empirical results provided in Panel A and B of Table 5.7, we find that the average economic benefit in the CNY is 271.8 bps in Period 1 and it rises sharply to 1679.9 bps in Period 2. Panel C shows that the average economic benefit in CNH is 324.8 bps. Although the economic benefits in the CNH are much smaller than CNY cases, the empirical results also indicate that hedging CNH currency risks is effective in Period 2.

Table 5.6 Sharpe ratios for optimal-weighted portfolios.

Dataset	S-B	S-I	S-O	Ind	Mom	Rev	ETF1	ETF2	ETF3	ETF0	Average
Panel A: Period 1 (CNY)											
Fully hedged	−0.0016	−0.0401	0.0463	−0.0649	−0.0926	−0.0659	−0.1963	0.0041	−0.0247	−0.0305	−0.0466
Unhedged	−0.0046	−0.0424	0.0360	−0.0745	−0.1052	−0.0563	−0.1952	−0.0152	−0.0298	−0.0430	−0.0530
Difference	0.0030	0.0023	0.0103	0.0095	0.0126	−0.0096	−0.0011	0.0193	0.0051	0.0125	0.0064
p-value	(0.2985)	(0.3247)	(0.0869)	(0.1048)	(0.0972)	(0.8008)	(0.5646)	(0.1723)	(0.2578)	(0.2245)	–
Panel B: Period 2 (CNY)											
Fully hedged	0.2849	0.3285	0.2588	0.2717	0.2987	0.2345	0.3222	0.3969	0.3854	0.2724	0.3054
Unhedged	0.0915	0.1305	0.0550	0.1389	0.1338	0.0427	0.1762	0.1239	0.1726	0.0883	0.1153
Difference	0.1934	0.1980	0.2038	0.1329	0.1649	0.1918	0.1460	0.2730	0.2128	0.1841	0.1901
p-value	(0.0000)	(0.0000)	(0.0001)	(0.0006)	(0.0000)	(0.0000)	(0.0001)	(0.0005)	(0.0018)	(0.0060)	–
Panel C: Period 2 (CNH)											
Fully hedged	0.1497	0.1757	0.1030	0.1702	0.1673	0.0948	0.2140	0.2668	0.2531	0.2061	0.1801
Unhedged	0.0933	0.1320	0.0559	0.1483	0.1337	0.0440	0.1764	0.1090	0.1665	0.0826	0.1142
Difference	0.0564	0.0438	0.0472	0.0220	0.0337	0.0508	0.0376	0.1578	0.0866	0.1235	0.0659
p-value	(0.0004)	(0.0021)	(0.0045)	(0.0508)	(0.0031)	(0.0003)	(0.0040)	(0.0020)	(0.0007)	(0.0007)	–

Table 5.7 Economic benefit for optimal-weighted portfolios.

Dataset	S-B	S-I	S-O	Ind	Mom	Rev	ETF1	ETF2	ETF3	ETF0	Average
Panel A: Period 1 (CNY)											
$\gamma = 1$	289.5	278.8	277.9	288.1	270.1	275.5	273.9	258.0	241.8	258.6	271.2
$\gamma = 5$	291.2	279.4	278.7	282.6	266.1	264.2	281.3	257.6	232.1	284.9	271.8
$\gamma = 10$	291.5	279.5	278.9	281.4	265.2	261.7	283.0	257.5	229.9	290.8	271.9
Panel B: Period 2 (CNY)											
$\gamma = 1$	1649.3	1645.1	1621.8	1575.5	1651.3	1702.2	1757.3	1765.0	1742.1	1747.1	1685.7
$\gamma = 5$	1639.6	1630.5	1613.0	1559.5	1631.5	1708.9	1752.4	1774.6	1737.3	1751.6	1679.9
$\gamma = 10$	1637.4	1627.2	1611.1	1555.8	1626.9	1710.4	1751.3	1776.8	1736.2	1752.7	1678.6
Panel C: Period 2 (CNH)											
$\gamma = 1$	324.6	319.6	315.4	251.6	361.1	296.0	22.5	330.2	310.5	410.0	324.2
$\gamma = 5$	327.6	321.2	315.8	241.6	356.3	295.4	327.6	334.6	308.7	418.7	324.8
$\gamma = 10$	328.3	321.5	315.9	239.4	355.2	295.2	328.8	335.6	308.3	420.8	324.9

Table 5.7 reports the economic benefits of fully hedged and unhedged portfolios based on the optimal-weighted strategy. Given the estimation window length is $M = 100$ and maximum allocation of each asset is 1, the optimal weights are estimated by achieving the maximum expected utility defined as Equation 5.13 or 5.14. Using these optimal weights to find the portfolio return at next period and this process is continued from $t = M + 1$. Therefore, the optimal-weighted portfolio returns are available. We report the estimates of Δ by Equation 5.16 as the annualized economic benefit in basis points using three different values of γ: 1, 5, and 10. In Panel A, the sample period is from 2 January 2006 to 7 September 2010; we use CNY and its forward CNYF to account for the currency risks and compute the fully hedged and unhedged portfolio returns. Similarly, in Panel B or C, the sample period is from 8 September 2010 to 31 December 2014; CNY (CNYF) and CNH (CNHF) are considered. In the last column are the average economic benefits among ten datasets.

5.3.4 Further evidence

The efficient frontiers and the time-varying rolling estimations are provided to further prove the effects of currency hedging.

5.3.4.1 Mean-variance frontiers

Based on equal-weighted strategy, the mean-variance frontiers for the fully hedged and unhedged portfolios are plotted in Figure 5.4. We discuss the frontiers for two datasets, DS(Ind) and DS(ETF0) in Periods 1 and 2, due to the frontiers' similar characteristics. In Figure 5.4, the return curves of fully hedged portfolios are represented by solid lines, and dashed lines refer to the return curves of unhedged portfolios. Clearly, the returns of fully hedged portfolios are greater than those of unhedged ones and the difference between two frontiers becomes much larger in Period 2. Furthermore, the performances of fully hedging for the CNY are much better than for the CNH.

This figure plots the mean-variance efficient frontiers for two datasets, DS(Ind) and DS(ETF0), which are based on the equal-weighted strategy. In the sample Period 1, from 2 January 2006 to 8 September 2010, the currency risk is estimated by CNY and is hedged by CNYF. In the sample Period 2, from 9 September 2010 to 31 December 2014, both CNY and CNH are considered.

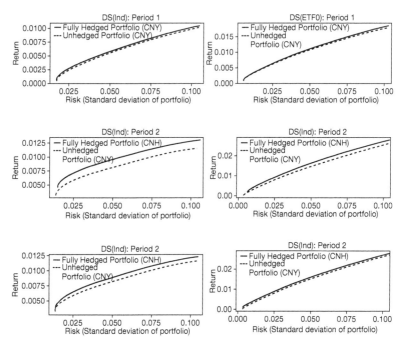

Figure 5.4 Efficient frontiers of fully hedged and unhedged portfolios.

5.3.4.2 Time-varying rolling estimations

In Section 5.3.1 (Data and statistics descriptions), we divide the full period into two sub-periods to analyze the before-and-after RMB liberalizations. Although this dividing method is a bit subjective, it still retains the main features of the data. Therefore, the time-varying rolling estimations, including Sharpe ratios and economic benefits, are introduced to measure the effects of fully hedging during the RMB internationalizing period. Considering the Sharpe ratio of a fully hedged case based on the equal-weighted strategy, we define the rolling window as 100 weeks at time t; then a rolling Sharpe ratio $SR_{H,t}$ can be calculated by $R_{H,t-99}$, $R_{H,t-98}$,..., $R_{H,t}$. Therefore, time-varying Sharpe ratios are generated by repeating the process from $t = M$ to T. Similarly, we can get rolling economic benefits. The time trends in rolling Sharpe ratios and the annualized economic benefit of fully hedged portfolios are provided in Figures 5.5 and 5.6, respectively. Clearly, both of the time-varying rolling estimations illustrate that fully hedging currency risk is effective.

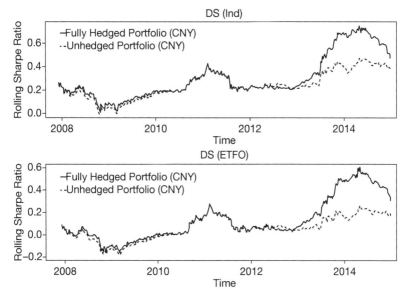

Figure 5.5 Time trends in rolling Sharpe ratios.

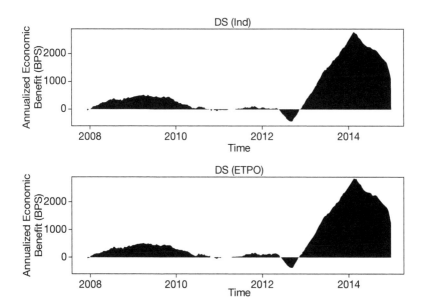

Figure 5.6 Annualized economic benefit of fully hedged portfolio.

Figure 5.5 plots rolling Sharpe ratios, based on 100-week windows, of the fully hedged and unhedged portfolios which consist of the dataset DS(Ind) and measure currency risk by CNY. Figure 5.6 below is similar, but considers the other dataset, DS(ETF0). Both sub-figures are based on the equal-weighted strategy. The sample covers weekly data; the period ranges from 2 January 2006 to 31 December 2014.

The annualized economic benefit of a fully hedged portfolio, which is estimated by the economic benefits between the fully hedged and unhedged portfolio, is based on 100-week rolling windows. This figure uses two datasets, DS(Ind) and DS(ETF0), with the equal-weighted strategy. Moreover, we set the risk aversion parameter, $\gamma = 5$, and use the CNY to cover the currency risk. The sample covers weekly data; the period ranges from 2 January 2006 to 31 December 2014.

5.4 Conclusion

We consider both CNY and CNH exchange rates and use the corresponding one-week RMB non-deliverable forwards to manage currency risk. This chapter studies the importance of hedging RMB risk during the RMB internationalizing period, which not only benefits Chinese institutions and individual investors, but also benefits individuals who possess assets based on the RMB. Ten datasets and a certain percentage of risky assets decided by both equal and optimal-weighted strategies are applied to construct the fully hedged and unhedged portfolios. The empirical results indicate that the results of fully hedging the CNY and CNH are similar while the CNY indicates a better hedging performance than the CNH in the empirical period from 2006 to 2014.

Based on the equal-weighted strategy, the average differences of Sharpe ratios between fully hedged and unhedged portfolios in the CNY are 0.0081 and 0.0607 in Periods 1 and 2 presented in Table 5.4, which proves that the effects of fully hedging the RMB are positive. Based on the optimal-weighted strategy, the differences between fully hedged and unhedged portfolios are not significant in Period 1; while in Period 2, the empirical results show fully hedged portfolios have significantly positive differences compared to unhedged portfolios. Therefore, we conclude that fully hedged portfolios produce a better performance than unhedged portfolios in terms of Sharpe ratios.

In addition to the Sharpe ratio, we also apply the economic benefit, which means how much a risk-averse investor would be willing to pay to construct a fully hedged portfolio to estimate the effects of hedging. Based on the equal-weighted portfolios, for fully hedging the CNY, the economic benefits range from 128.5 to 143.7 bps in Period 1; in Period 2, the economic benefits in the CNY increase sharply, ranging from 726.3 to 810.9 bps. The economic benefits in the CNH range from 34.6 to 339.5 bps, shown in Table 5.5. Based on the optimal-weighted strategy, the empirical results also indicate investors are willing to pay higher fees to hedge currency risks.

Furthermore, the efficient frontiers and the time-varying rolling estimations are provided to further prove the effects of currency hedging. All empirical results mentioned above indicate that it is urgently necessary for Chinese investors who hold foreign assets in US dollars to hedge the RMB exchange rate. Especially during the RMB internationalizing, the volatility of the RMB exchange rate is greater and investors should pay more attention to RMB hedging.

Notes

1 This report shows that the gross domestic product, based on purchasing-power-parity valuation of the country GDP for China, is US$ 18.088 billion; by comparison, the United States' GDP is US$ 17.348 billion. The source website is www.imf.org/data.
2 Kroencke and Schindler (2012) apply the spanning test statistics; see Huberman and Kandel (1987) and Jobson and Korkie (1989), for a complete shift of the frontier when N assets are added to K benchmark assets. However, our empirical study compares only two frontiers without adding any assets; therefore we show only the mean-variance frontiers.
3 Although we focus on the perspective of Chinese investors in this paper, hedging RMB risk is equally important to international companies that use the RMB as the settlement currency or investors who hold some financial assets based on the RMB.
4 Besides the tables shown in this paper, we have also developed several robust tests with different parameter settings including the estimation window of length M=50, maximum allocation of each asset as 0.5, and the restriction of shorting assets. These robust experiments are used to evaluate the Sharpe ratios and economic benefit cases. All results indicate the same characteristic: currency hedging becomes more important when the RMB is internationalizing.

References

Abiad, A. G. (2003). Early warning systems: A survey and a regime-switching approach. *Social Science Electronic Publishing*, *3*(32), 993–1052.

Alexander, G. J., & Baptista, A. M. (2002). Economic implications of using a mean-VaR model for portfolio selection: A comparison with mean-variance analysis. *Journal of Economic Dynamics and Control*, *26*(7–8), 1159–1193.

Allayannis, G., & Ofek, E. (2001). Exchange rate exposure, hedging, and the use of foreign currency derivatives. *Journal of International Money & Finance*, *20*(2), 273–296.

Bandi, F. M., & Russell, J. R. (2006). Separating microstructure noise from volatility. *Journal of Financial Economics*, *79*(3), 655–692.

Barry, C. B. (1974). Portfolio analysis under uncertain means, variances, and covariances. *The Journal of Finance*, *29*(2), 515–522.

Bénassy-Quéré, A., & Forouheshfar, Y. (2015). The impact of yuan internationalization on the stability of the international monetary system. *Journal of International Money & Finance*, *57*(2), 115–135.

Berg, A. & Pattillo, C. (1999). Predicting currency crises: The indicators approach and an alternative. *Journal of International Money & Finance*, *18*(4), 561–586.

Brown, S. (1979). The effect of estimation risk on capital market equilibrium. *Journal of Financial and Quantitative Analysis*, *14*(2), 215–220.

Campbell, J. Y., Medeiros, S. D., & Visceira, L. M. (2010). Global currency hedging. *The Journal of Finance*, *65*(1), 87–121.

Cerra, V., & Saxena, S. C. (2002). Contagion, monsoons, and domestic turmoil in Indonesia's currency crisis. *Review of International Economics*, *10*(1), 36–44.

Chen, C. (2006). *Forecasting in Foreign Exchange Markets*. Davis, CA: University of California.

Chen, C. F., & Lai, M. C. & Yeh C. C. (2011). Forecasting tourism demand based on empirical mode decomposition and neural network. *Knowledge-Based Systems*. *26*, 281–287.

Cheung, Y. W., & Rime, D. (2014). The offshore renminbi exchange rate: Microstructure and links to the onshore market. *Journal of International Money & Finance*, *49*, 170–189.

Craig, R.S., Hua, C., Ng, P. K., & Yuen, R. (2013). Development of the renminbi market in Hong Kong SAR: Assessing onshore-offshore market integration. IMF Working Paper 13/268. Retrieved from https://www.imf.org/external/pubs/ft/wp/2013/wp13268.pdf

Cui, Y. (2014). Revisiting China's exchange rate regime and RMB basket: A recent empirical study. *RSC Advances*, *6*(2), 21575.

DeMiguel V., Garlappi, L., & Uppal, R. (2009). Optimal versus naive diversification: How inefficient is the 1/N portfolio strategy? *Review of Financial Studies*, *22*(5), 1915–1953.

Eun, C. S., & Resnick, B. G. (1988). Exchange rate uncertainty, forward contracts, and international portfolio selection. *The Journal of Finance*, *43*(1), 197–215.

Fleming, J., Kirby, C., & Ostdiek, B. (2001). The economic value of volatility timing. *The Journal of Finance*, *56*(1), 329–352.

Fleming, J., Kirby, C., & Ostdiek, B. (2003). The economic value of volatility timing using "realized" volatility. *Journal of Financial Economics*, *67*(3), 473–509.

Fratzscher, M., & Mehl, A. (2014). China's dominance hypothesis and the emergence of a tri-polar global currency system. *The Economic Journal*, *124*(581), 1343–1370.

French, K. (2014). *Kenneth R. French – Data Library*. Retrieved from http://mba.tuck.dartmouth.edu/pages/faculty/ken.french/data_library.html

Funke, M., & Shu, C., Cheng, X., & Eraslan, S. (2015). Assessing the CNH-CNY pricing differential: Role of fundamentals, contagion and policy. *Journal of International Money Finance*, *59*(6), 245–262.

Gatopoulos, G., & Loubergé, H. (2013). Combined use of foreign debt and currency derivatives under the threat of currency crises: The case of Latin American firms. *Journal of International Money & Finance*, *35*(2), 54–75.

Glen, J., & Jorion, P. (1993). Currency hedging for international portfolios. *The Journal of Finance*, 48(5), 1865–1886.

Günther, F, & Fritsch, S. (2010). neuralnet: Training of neural networks. *The R Journal, 2*(1), 30–38.

Hamilton, J. D. (1994). Modeling time series with changes in regime. In Hamilton, J. *Time Series Analysis* (pp. 677–703). Princeton, NJ: Princeton University Press.

Henning, C. R. (2012). Choice and coercion in East Asian exchange rate regimes. Working Paper 12-15. Washington, DC: Peterson Institute for International Economics. Retrieved from https://piie.com/publications/wp/wp12-15.pdf

Hornik, K., Stinchcombe, M., & White, H. (1989). Multilayer feedforward networks are universal approximators. *Neural Networks*, *2*(5), 359–366.

Hossfeld, O., & Macdonald, R. (2015). Carry funding and safe haven currencies: A threshold regression approach. *Journal of International Money & Finance*, *59*, 185–202.

Huang, N. E., & Shen Z., Long, S. R., Wu, M. C., Shih, H. H., Zheng Q... Liu, H. H. (1998). The empirical mode decomposition and the Hilbert spectrum for nonlinear and non-stationary time series analysis. *Proceedings of the Royal Society A Mathematical Physical and Engineering Sciences*, *454*(1971), 903–995.

Huang, N. E., Shen, Z., & Long, S. R. (1999). A new view of nonlinear water waves: the Hilbert Spectrum. *Annual Review of Fluid Mechanics, 31*(1), 417–457.

Huang, N. E., Wu M. L. C., & Long, S. R. (2003). A confidence limit for the empirical mode decomposition and Hilbert spectral analysis. *Proceedings of the Royal Society A Mathematical Physical and Engineering Sciences, 459*(2037), 2317–2345.

Huang, W., Lai, K. K., Nakamori, Y., & Wang, S. Y. (2003). An empirical analysis of sampling interval for exchange rate forecasting with neural networks. *Journal of Systems Science and Complexity, 16*(2), 165–176.

Huang X., Wu, C. (2006). Interaction between onshore spot rate and offshore non-deliverable forward: Before and after reform. *Journal of Financial Research, 51*(11), 83–89.

International Monetary Fund (2016). *IMF launches new SDR basket including Chinese renminbi, determines new currency amounts* [Press release No. 16/440]. Retrieved from http://www.imf.org/en/News/Articles/2016/09/30/AM16-PR16440-IMF-Launches-New-SDR-Basket-Including-Chinese-Renminbi

Jobson, J. D. & Korkie, B. M. (1981) Performance hypothesis testing with the Sharpe and Treynor measures. *The Journal of Finance, 36*(4), 889–908.

Jorion, P. (1994). Mean/variance analysis of currency overlays. *Financial Analysts Journal, 50*(3), 48–56.

Kaminsky, G., Reinhart, C. M., & Lizondo S. (1998). Leading indicators of currency crises. *IMF Economic Review, 45*(1), 1–48.

Khashei, M., Bijari, M., & Ardali, G. A. R. (2009). Improvement of auto-regressive integrated moving average models using Fuzzy logic and artificial neural networks (ANNs). *Neurocomputing, 72*(4–6), 956–967.

Klein, R. W., & Bawa,. V. S. (1976). The effect of estimation risk on optimal portfolio choice. *Journal of Financial Economics, 3*, 215–231.

Kroencke, T. A., & Schindler F. (2012). International diversification with securitized real estate and the veiling glare from currency risk. *Journal of International Money & Finance, 31*(7), 1851–1866.

Lin, C. S., Chiu, S. H., & Lin, T. Y. (2012). Empirical mode decomposition–based least squares support vector regression for foreign exchange rate forecasting. *Economic Modelling, 29*(6), 2583–2590.

Lustig, H., & Verdelhan, A. (2007). The cross section of foreign currency risk premia and consumption growth risk. *The American Economic Review, 97*(1), 89–117.

Lustig, H., Roussanov N., & Verdelhan, A. (2011). Common risk factors in currency markets. *Review of Financial Studies, 24*(11), 3731–3777.

MacKinlay, A. C., & Pástor, Ľ. (2000). Asset pricing models: Implications for expected returns and portfolio selection. *The Review of Financial Studies, 13*(4), 883–916.

Pástor, L., & Stambaugh R. F. (2000). Comparing asset pricing models: An investment perspective.

Peroldandre, F., & Schulmanevan C. (1988). The free lunch in currency hedging, implications for investment policy and peformance standards. *Financial Analysts Journal, 44*(3), 45–50.

Prasad, E. S., & Ye L. (2011). The Renminbi's role in the global monetary system. *Iza Discussion Papers*, *11*, 199–206.

Riedmiller, M., & Braun H. (1993). *A direct adaptive method for faster back-propagation learning: The RPROP algorithm*. IEEE International Conference on Neural Networks, San Francisco, CA, USA.

Rojas, R. (1996, 2013). *Neural networks: A systematic introduction.* Berlin, Germany: Springer Science & Business Media.

Shu, C., He, D., & Cheng, Z. (2015). One currency, two markets: The renminbi's growing influence in Asia-Pacific. *China Economic Review*, *33*, 163–178.

Subramanian, A., & Kessler, M. (2014). The renminbi bloc is here: Asia down, rest of the world to go? *Working Paper*, *4*(1), 49–94.

Verdelhan, A. (2012). The Share of Systematic Variation in Bilateral Exchange Rates. 2012 Meeting Papers, Society for Economic Dynamics. Retrieved from https://economicdynamics.org/meetpapers/2012/paper_763.pdf

Wei, O., & Dark J. (2015). Currency overlay for global equity portfolios: Cross-hedging and base currency. *Journal of Futures Markets*, *35*(2), 186–200.

Yan, M., & Ba, S. (2010). The dynamic relationship among RMB spot exchange rate, onshore forward exchange rate and offshore forward exchange rate after the implementation of NDF regulation policy. *Journal of Finance & Economics*, Vol. 2010-02. Beijing: China Knowledge Institute (CNKI).

Yu, L., Lai K. K., Wang, S., & He, K. (2007, May 27–30). *Oil price forecasting with an EMD-based multiscale neural network learning paradigm*. Proceedings of the International Conference on Computational Science - Iccs 2007, Beijing, China.

Yu, L., Wang, S., & Lai, K. K. (2005). A novel nonlinear ensemble forecasting model incorporating GLAR and ANN for foreign exchange rates *Computers & Operations Research*, *32*(10), 2523–2541.

Yu, L., Wang, S., & Lai, K. K. (2008). Forecasting crude oil price with an EMD-based neural network ensemble learning paradigm. *Energy Economics*, *30*(5), 2623–2635.

Yu, L., Wang, S., & Lai, K. K. (2010). *Foreign-Exchange-Rate Forecasting with Artificial Neural Networks* (Vol. 107). Berlin, Germany: Springer Science & Business Media.

Zhang, G. P. (2001). An investigation of neural networks for linear time-series forecasting. *Computers & Operations Research*, *28*(12), 1183–1202.

Zhang, G., Patuwo, B. E., & Hu, M. Y. (1998). Forecasting with artificial neural networks: The state of the art. *International Journal of Forecasting*, *14*(1): 35–62.

Zhou, S., & Lai, K. K. (2011). An Improved EMD Online Learning-Based Model for Gold Market Forecasting. In: Watada J., Phillips-Wren G., Jain L. C., & Howlett R. J. (Eds.) *Smart Innovation, Systems and Technologies (SIST): Vol. 10. Intelligent Decision Technologies: Proceedings of the 3rd International Conference on Intelligent Decision Technologies* (IDT 2011, pp. 75–84). Berlin, Heidelberg: Springer.

Index

For Product Safety Concerns and Information please contact our EU
representative GPSR@taylorandfrancis.com
Taylor & Francis Verlag GmbH, Kaufingerstraße 24, 80331 München, Germany

www.ingramcontent.com/pod-product-compliance
Ingram Content Group UK Ltd.
Pitfield, Milton Keynes, MK11 3LW, UK
UKHW021838240425
457818UK00007B/227